ACCA

F4   CORPORATE AND BUSINESS LAW

(ENGLISH)

REVISION QUESTION BANK

For Examinations from September 2017 to August 2018

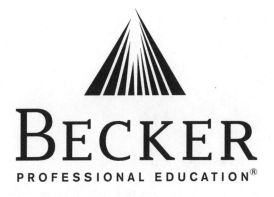

BECKER

PROFESSIONAL EDUCATION®

Acknowledgement

Past ACCA examination questions are the copyright of the Association of Chartered Certified Accountants and have been reproduced by kind permission.

Becker Professional Education, a global leader in professional education, has been developing study materials for the ACCA for more than 20 years. Thousands of students studying for the ACCA Qualification have succeeded in their professional examinations studying with its Platinum and Gold ALP training centers in Central and Eastern Europe and Central Asia.

Nearly half a million professionals have advanced their careers through Becker Professional Education's courses. Throughout its 60-year history, Becker has earned a strong track record of student success through world-class teaching, curriculum and learning tools.

Becker Professional Education has been awarded ACCA Approved Content Provider Status for its ACCA materials, as well as materials for the Diploma in International Financial Reporting (DipIFR).

We provide a single solution for individuals and companies in need of global accounting certifications and continuing professional education.

Becker Professional Education's ACCA Study Materials

All of Becker's materials are authored by experienced ACCA lecturers and are used in the delivery of classroom courses.

Study Text: Gives complete coverage of the syllabus with a focus on learning outcomes. It is designed to be used both as a reference text and as part of integrated study. It also includes the ACCA Syllabus and Study Guide, exam advice and commentaries and a Study Question Bank containing practice questions relating to each topic covered.

Revision Question Bank: Exam style and standard questions together with comprehensive answers to support and prepare students for their exams. The Revision Question Bank also includes past examination questions (updated where relevant), model answers and alternative solutions and tutorial notes.

Revision Essentials Handbook*: A condensed, easy-to-use aid to revision containing essential technical content and exam guidance.

*Revision Essentials Handbook are substantially derived from content reviewed by ACCA's examining team.

Becker Professional Education
is an ACCA approved content provider

CONTENTS

Question		Page	Answer	Marks	Date worked

MULTIPLE CHOICE QUESTIONS

1	English legal system	1	1001	26	
2	Tort law	4	1002	35	
3	Elements of contract law	8	1003	30	
4	Contract law – terms	11	1004	28	
5	Contract law – breach	15	1005	40	
6	Employment law	20	1007	31	
7	Agency	23	1008	26	
8	Partnership	26	1009	28	
9	Corporations and legal personality	29	1010	16	
10	Company formation	31	1010	28	
11	Memorandum and articles	35	1011	15	
12	Share capital	37	1012	15	
13	Capital maintenance and dividends	38	1013	27	
14	Loan capital	41	1014	22	
15	Company directors	44	1014	23	
16	Other company officers	47	1015	18	
17	Company meetings and resolutions	49	1016	21	
18	Insolvency and administration	51	1017	36	
19	Fraudulent and criminal behaviour	55	1018	34	

Section B of the Examination will include only six mark questions (see Specimen Exam).
All past exam questions shown below have been adapted.

TORT LAW

1	Bizzy Ltd	59	1020	6	
2	Professor Parfitt	59	1020	6	
3	Gregory, Douglas and Michael	59	1021	6	
4	Escapade Ltd	60	1021	6	
5	Netscape Ltd and Netscope Ltd	60	1022	6	

ELEMENTS OF CONTRACT LAW

6	Helen & Ingrid	60	1022	6	
7	Alan *(ACCA D04)*	61	1023	6	
8	Al & Bash Cars plc *(ACCA Pilot D07)*	61	1024	6	
9	Ami *(ACCA J10)*	61	1024	6	
10	Amy & Ben Che *(ACCA D10)*	62	1025	6	
11	Ade *(ACCA D11)*	62	1025	6	
12	Ali *(ACCA D12)*	63	1026	6	
13	Ano Ltd *(ACCA J13)*	63	1027	6	

CONTRACT LAW – TERMS

14	Abid *(ACCA D13)*	63	1027	6	

Question		Page	Answer	Marks	Date worked
CONTRACT LAW – BREACH					
15	Andre *(ACCA J05)*	64	1028	6	
16	Ari, Bi & Cas *(ACCA J11)**	64	1029	6	
17	AZ Ltd *(ACCA J12)*	65	1029	6	
18	Apt Ltd *(ACCA J14)*	65	1030	6	
EMPLOYMENT LAW					
19	Dai & Chris	65	1030	6	
20	Fitz *(ACCA J06)*	66	1031	6	
21	Dan *(ACCA J12)*	66	1032	6	
AGENCY					
22	Goal Ltd *(ACCA J11)**	67	1032	6	
PARTNERSHIP					
23	Chi, Di & Fi *(ACCA J10)*	67	1033	6	
24	Geo, Ho & Io *(ACCA D10)*	67	1034	6	
25	Han, Ita & Jo *(ACCA J13)*	68	1035	6	
CORPORATIONS AND LEGAL PERSONALITY					
26	Frank *(ACCA J00)*	68	1036	6	
27	Doc *(ACCA D11)**	69	1036	6	
COMPANY FORMATION					
28	Don *(ACCA J05)*	69	1037	6	
MEMORANDUM AND ARTICLES					
29	Fred *(ACCA D08)*	69	1038	6	
SHARE CAPITAL					
30	Gilt Ltd *(ACCA J10)*	70	1038	10	
CAPITAL MAINTENANCE AND DIVIDENDS					
31	Dee & Eff *(ACCA D10)*	70	1039	10	
LOAN CAPITAL					
32	Hot Ltd *(ACCA D13)*	71	1039	6	

* See Tutorial note to the Specimen and December 2014 Exams on page (vi).

Question		Page	Answer	Marks	Date worked
COMPANY DIRECTORS					
33	Clean Ltd *(ACCA J09)*	71	1040	6	
34	Caz *(ACCA D09)*	72	1041	6	
35	Just Ltd *(ACCA J12)*	72	1041	6	
36	Fay, Gus and Het *(ACCA D12)*	72	1042	6	
37	Dix plc *(ACCA J14)*	73	1042	6	
38	IMP Ltd *(ACCA J14)*	73	1043	6	
OTHER COMPANY OFFICERS					
39	Mavi Ltd	74	1043	6	
40	Dee, Fi, Gee & Ki *(ACCA J13)*	74	1044	6	
41	Chu *(ACCA D13)*	75	1045	6	
COMPANY MEETINGS AND RESOLUTIONS					
42	Loss plc *	75	1045	6	
INSOLVENCY AND ADMINISTRATION					
43	Earl *(ACCA D07)*	75	1046	6	
44	Mat, Mary & Norm *(ACCA J11)*	76	1047	6	
FRAUDULENT AND CRIMINAL BEHAVIOUR					
45	Jason	76	1047	6	
46	Large plc *(ACCA Pilot D07)*	77	1048	6	
47	Ian *(ACCA D11)*	77	1049	6	
48	Jaz plc *(ACCA D12)*	78	1050	6	

Tutorial note: *The suggested answers to the above may include details of decided cases and statutes that are in addition to the details provided in the F4 Study Text. These and other details provided in tutorial notes are not necessary for a candidate to succeed in passing exam questions as illustrated by the Specimen Exam.*

Question		Page	Answer	Marks	Date worked
SPECIMEN EXAM (applicable from December 2014) *					
Section A	45 Multiple Choice Questions	2	17	70	
Section B	5 Multi-Task Questions				
1	Az Ltd	12	17	6	
2	Clare, Dan and Eve	12	18	6	
3	Jon	13	18	6	
4	Ger and Kim	13	18	6	
5	Fran and Gram	14	18	6	
	Marking Scheme		19		
DECEMBER 2014 EXAM					
Section A	45 Multiple Choice Questions	2	15	70	
Section B	5 Multi-Task Questions				
1	Ann, Con and Di	11	15	6	
2	Glad Ltd	11	16	6	
3	Ho, Ice and Jet	12	16	6	
4	Kut Ltd	12	17	6	
5	Nit, Owen and Pat	12	17	6	
	Marking Scheme		19		

Tutorial notes:

The above exams include a few 1 mark multiple choice questions requiring analysis; 6, 12, 18 and 25 in the Specimen and 5, 16, 19 and 31 in the December exam. ACCA advises that such questions would now be 2 marks with an option D; 1 mark questions will be pure knowledge questions.

Multi-task questions in computer-based examinations will have parts with 2 marks and 4 marks only, as illustrated by the Specimen and December 2014 Exams. Paper-based examinations could, however, include parts with 3 marks as illustrated by some of the Section B questions in this question bank.

---

* If you are preparing to sit the computer-based exam it is essential that you attempt the CBE Specimen available at http://specimen.accaglobal.com/fls.html.

MCQs 1 ENGLISH LEGAL SYSTEM

1.1 **Which of the following statements about the aim of the criminal law is accurate?**

    A   It is to regulate behaviour within society by the threat of punishment

    B   It is to provide a means whereby injured persons may obtain compensation

    C   It is to ensure that the will of the majority is imposed upon the minority   (1 mark)

1.2 **Which of the following is associated with private law?**

    A   Constitution law

    B   Criminal law

    C   Insolvency law   (1 mark)

1.3 **Which rule of interpretation requires the interpretation in the ordinary sense of words unless that would lead to some absurdity?**

    A   The golden rule

    B   The literal rule

    C   The mischief rule   (1 mark)

1.4 **Which of the following courts in the English systems has criminal jurisdiction?**

    A   Divisional Court

    B   County Court

    C   Crown Court   (1 mark)

1.5 **Which of the following describes a statement that is made *obiter dicta*?**

    A   It is binding in certain courts hearing similar disputes

    B   It is not binding unless made by the House of Lords

    C   It is a principle of law which relate to the facts of the dispute upon which the decision is based

    D   It is not binding on any later court determining a similar dispute but may be regarded as judicial authority   (2 marks)

1.6 **Which of the following terms is used to describe the reasoning behind a judicial decision?**

    A   Per incuriam

    B   Obiter dicta

    C   Ratio decidendi   (1 mark)

1.7 **Which of the following terms is used to describe the person against whom a case is brought?**

    A   Prosecution

    B   Defendent

    C   Plaintiff   (1 mark)

1.8   Which of the following statements relating to equity is correct?

(1)   An Act of Parliament can overrule any common law or equitable rule

(2)   The concept of damages for harm suffered in consequence of wrongdoing is a feature of equity

A   1 only
B   2 only
C   Neither 1 nor 2
D   Both 1 and 2   (2 marks)

1.9   In which court do all criminal cases commence?

A   The County Court
B   The Crown Court
C   The Magistrates Court   (1 mark)

1.10   When does a Parliamentary Bill become an Act of Parliament?

A   When it passes through the committee stage
B   On receiving its third reading
C   On receiving the Royal Assent   (1 mark)

1.11   Which rule of interpretation involves an examination of the former law in an attempt to deduce Parliament's intention?

A   The golden rule
B   The literal rule
C   The mischief rule   (1 mark)

1.12   What does "overruling" mean?

A   A lower court disagrees with the original decision made by a higher court
B   A higher court overturns the original decision of a lower court
C   A higher court agrees with the original decision of a lower court in the same case   (1 mark)

1.13   Gordon was injured when a piece of scaffolding fell on him and struck his shoulder. He wants to claim £2,500 for personal injury.

Can Gordon use the small claims track and why?

A   Yes – Claims for amounts less than £10,000 always fall within the small claims track

B   No – Personal injury claims never fall within the small claims track

C   No – Claims for personal injury worth more than £1,000 do not fall within the small claims track

D   No – Personal injury claims for less than £10,000 must be settled by negotiation between the parties and are not a matter for the courts   (2 marks)

1.14   To which court is an appeal made from the Employment Appeal Tribunal?

A   Crown Court
B   The Court of Appeal
C   Supreme Court   (1 mark)

1.15 **What is the normal standard of proof placed upon the prosecution in a CRIMINAL case?**

A	Balance of probabilities	
B	Beyond every reasonable doubt	
C	Beyond reasonable doubt	(1 mark)

1.16 **Which of the following statements best describes a directive passed by the Council of Ministers of the European Union?**

A	It is self-executing and applies to all member states at once	
B	It would require further legislation to be passed before becoming law	
C	It would become law automatically after a certain period of time	(1 mark)

1.17 **Which of the following presumptions are valid when interpreting legislation?**

(1)	Statutes operate retrospectively	
(2)	The Crown is not bound by the statute	
(3)	The statute does not intend to deprive a person of his liberty	

A	1 and 2 only	
B	1 and 3 only	
C	2 and 3 only	
D	1, 2 and 3	(2 marks)

1.18 **Which of the following statements is the *ratio decidendi*?**

A	The legal reasoning behind the decision	
B	Something said in a dissenting judgment	
C	Speculation on the outcome of the case if the facts had been different	(1 mark)

1.19 **Which of the following statements about European Union Law is correct?**

A	European Union Law takes precedence over domestic law	
B	Domestic law takes precedence over European Union law	
C	Treaties among member states of the European Community are not highly priotised in European Union law	(1 mark)

1.20 **In the context of the English system, which of the following courts would hear family law appeals from the magistrates' court and county courts?**

A	Crown court	
B	Administrative court	
C	Divisional court	(1 mark)

1.21 The Civil Procedure Rules 1998 apply to the courts when dealing with civil cases.

What is the overriding objective of these rules?

A	To ensure that the parties are on an equal footing	
B	To deal with cases justly and at a proportionate cost	
C	To ensure that cases are dealt with expeditiously and fairly	
D	To enforce compliance with rules, practice directions and orders	(2 marks)

(26 marks)

MCQs 2 TORT LAW

2.1 **What is the standard of care applied to professionals with a special skill or expertise?**

A   That of the reasonable person with the same skill or expertise

B   That of the reasonable person in the same general profession

C   That of the reasonable person

D   That of the reasonable person with the same level of experience in that skill or expertise   (2 marks)

2.2 **In accordance with *Caparo Industries v Dickman (1990)*, which of the following must be considered by the court to establish whether a duty of care exists?**

A   Reasonable foresight of harm and sufficient proximity of relationship

B   Any harm, reasonable proximity of relationship and that it is just, fair and reasonable to impose a duty

C   Reasonable foresight of harm, reasonable proximity of relationship and that it is just, fair and reasonable to impose a duty

D   Reasonable foresight of harm, sufficient proximity of relationship and that it is just, fair and reasonable to impose a duty   (2 marks)

2.3 **Which of the following factors must be present for *res ipsa loquitur* to be available to assist a claimant?**

(1)   The claimant must have suffered physical injury

(2)   The thing causing the damage is under the control of the defendant or someone for whose negligence the defendant is responsible

(3)   The accident is such as would not normally occur without negligence

(4)   The cause of the accident is unknown

A   1, 2 and 3

B   1, 2 and 4

C   1, 3 and 4

D   2, 3 and 4   (2 marks)

2.4 **When do acts of nature break the chain of causation?**

A   Always

B   Where they are unforeseeable but linked to the original negligent act or omission

C   Where they are unforeseeable and separate from the original negligent act or omission   (1 mark)

2.5 **What does the "eggshell skull" rule mean?**

A   That defendants are not liable if their victims have head injuries

B   That defendants must take their victims as they find them

C   That defendants are only liable for the injuries that a reasonably fit person would suffer   (1 mark)

2.6 **When is economic loss recoverable in tort?**

A   When it is purely economic loss

B   Whenever economic loss is suffered

C   When it is caused by the acquisition of defective goods or property

D   When it is caused by damage to property   (2 marks)

2.7 **Which of the following could constitute a "special relationship" for the purposes of negligent misstatement?**

A	Parent and (adult) child	
B	Environmental health inspector and hotelier	
C	Banker and client	
D	Husband and wife	(2 marks)

2.8 **Which of the following relationships may give rise to vicarious liability?**

(1) Vehicle owners and delegated drivers
(2) Employer and employee
(3) Teachers and pupils in their care during school hours

A	1 and 2	
B	1 and 3	
C	2 and 3	(1 mark)

2.9 **Which TWO of the following statements have the meaning of the defence *volenti non fit injuria*?**

A	There is a voluntary assumption of risk
B	There can be no injury to one who consents
C	A person who causes injury must be held liable
D	Punishment should fit the violence of the injury caused

A	1 and 2	
B	1 and 4	
C	2 and 3	
D	3 and 4	(2 marks)

2.10 Aaron bought a bottle of a soft drink. He noticed a jagged piece of glass at the top of the bottle. Aaron decided to use a glass cutter to remove the jagged piece of glass and cut himself very badly.

Damages awarded to him may be reduced because of which of the following?

A	Volenti non fit injuria	
B	Res ipsa loquitur	
C	Contributory negligence	
D	Breach of duty of care	(2 marks)

2.11 **Which TWO of the following statements regarding the defence of consent are true?**

(1) A defence of *volenti non fit injuria* will fail if the claimant had no choice other than to consent to the risk

(2) A person who gets into a car with a drunken or inexperienced driver consents to the risk of injury during the journey

(3) A fireman injured as a result of a broken ladder during a fire rescue will not be viewed as giving free consent

(4) Consent and contributory negligence have so much in common that they are essentially the same defence and have the same effect if argued successfully by the defendant

A	1 and 2
B	1 and 3
C	2 and 4
D	3 and 4

(2 marks)

2.12   What is the effect of a successful claim of contributory negligence?

A   The claimant is found to be responsible for his own injuries so his claim is dismissed

B   The claimant is partially responsible for his own injuries thus his level of damages is reduced

C   The defendant is found to be the only cause of the claimant's injuries and will therefore have to pay compensation

D   The claimant is found to be responsible for his own injuries and must therefore compensate the defendant for bringing the action against him   (2 marks)

2.13   In which of the following situations will a defendant be liable for their negligence?

A   If the loss would have occurred regardless of the defendant's negligence

B   If but for his negligence the loss or damage would not have occurred

C   If there is *novus actus interveniens*   (1 mark)

2.14   Michael visited the Seaview Marine Centre. While looking at the sea-lions' pool, he saw a little girl drop her teddy bear over the barrier and into the water. Michael crossed the barrier, ignored a warning sign and reached into the water to rescue the bear but was badly bitten on his arm by two sea-lions. He wishes to claim damages.

What is the legal position?

A   The Marine Centre will have no liability to Michael as there was no immediate danger and he was under no legal or moral pressure to rescue the bear

B   The Marine Centre will be liable to pay damages to Michael as he was not adequately warned of the danger of the sea-lions

C   The Marine Centre will be liable to pay damages to Michael as he was compelled to rescue the bear

D   The Marine Centre will have no liability to Michael as the incident was an inevitable accident   (2 marks)

2.15   What forms the basis of the existence of a legal duty of care in negligence for misstatements resulting in economic loss to the plaintiff?

(1)   Proximity between the parties
(2)   Reasonable foreseeability of damage

A   1 only
B   2 only
C   Neither 1 nor 2
D   Both 1 and 2   (2 marks)

2.16   Gerry drove his car negligently and mounted the pavement causing injury to Tom, a pedestrian. Although Tom's injuries were not serious they resulted in his being off work for six months because he suffered from a genetic blood disorder. Tom was a high-flying merchant banker and claims for loss of earnings of £350,000. Gerry disputes this claim as excessive.

In relation to the law of negligence, what is Gerry's liability?

A   Gerry is only liable for normal damages; Tom's disease is a *novus actus interveniens* and could not be foreseen

B   Gerry is liable for the full damages since he must take his victim as he finds him

C   Gerry will not be liable for the full damage; under the "eggshell skull rule" the presence of the serious blood disease could not have been foreseen

D   Gerry will only be liable for the damage which could have been foreseen; Tom's loss of earnings were special damages   (2 marks)

2.17   John, a learner driver, was taking lessons from friend, Steve. Before agreeing to be John's instructor, Steve checked that John's insurance covered him as a passenger. On one of the lessons John drove negligently and injured Steve.

What is John's duty of care in this case?

A   The same standard as a reasonable qualfied competent driver
B   That of any unqualified learner driver
C   That which might reasonably be expected of a similarly inexperienced driver
D   He has no duty of care as the defence of *volenti non fit injuria* applies

(2 marks)

2.18   **If the plaintiff was contributorily negligent, what effect does this have on a claim for damages for negligence?**

A   The defendant is not liable to pay damages
B   The amount of damages payable by the defendant is reduced
C   It has no effect on the award of damages
D   Both the plaintiff and the defendant must pay damages to each other   (2 marks)

2.19   **In relation to the law of contract, to whom does an auditor appointed under the provisions of the *Companies Act 2006* owe a duty?**

A   The company only
B   The company and the directors
C   The company and the shareholders   (1 mark)

2.20   **What does a claimant need to show to establish liability in a negligence claim?**

(1)   That they have suffered loss or injury
(2)   That they were owed a duty of care by the defendant
(3)   That the defendant caused them loss or injury

A   1 and 2 only
B   1 and 3 only
C   2 and 3 only
D   1, 2 and 3   (2 marks)

(35 marks)

MCQs 3 ELEMENTS OF CONTRACT LAW

3.1   Rosemary offered by letter to sell Mary her motorbike for £5,000. Mary wrote back saying she accepted the offer and would pay in two instalments at the end of the two following months.

Is there a contract and for what reason?

A   No – because Mary is trying to amend the contractual terms, Rosemary can be assumed to have revoked the offer

B   Yes – there has been an offer and acceptance and a binding contract exists

C   No – Mary's response constitutes a counter-offer and is effectively a rejection of Rosemary's offer

D   Yes – Mary's response is merely a clarification of contractual terms   (2 marks)

3.2   Tee Ltd placed some computers in its shop window with a notice which read: "Special offer. Internet-ready computers for sale at £400".

Which of the following is correct?

(1)   The notice amounts to an invitation to treat

(2)   When Anne called in to the shop and offered £350 for one of the computers, she had made a counter-offer

(3)   Tee Ltd is legally obliged to sell a computer to anyone who can pay the price

A   1 only
B   1 and 2 only
C   1 and 3 only
D   1, 2 and 3   (2 marks)

3.3   An offer was made by letter posted on 21 July and delivered on 27 July. A reply accepting the offer was e-mailed on 29 July and the acceptor received a delivery receipt on 30 July. The offeror read the reply on 4 August.

On which date was the contract made?

A   27 July
B   29 July
C   30 July
D   4 August   (2 marks)

3.4   Peter owed Kate £1,000. Peter's father, James, agreed with Kate, in writing, to pay her £550 if she took it "in full settlement". Kate took the £550 on this basis and then demanded £450 from Peter. Peter refused to pay.

In the context of contract law what is Peter's position?

A   Peter is liable – part payment of a debt is not consideration for a promise to discharge the debt

B   Peter is not liable – part payment of a debt by a third party is good consideration for a promise not to sue for the balance

C   Peter will be liable – James, as his father, is not a third party

D   Peter will not be liable – the agreement between Kate and James was in writing
                                                                              (2 marks)

3.5 Special Books Ltd sent Rose an offer for her to purchase a rare book. The offer had to be accepted within five days of the date on the letter. Rose intended to accept the offer and purchase the book.

Which of the following statements is true ?

A   Rose may have a legitimate claim if she faxed acceptance of the offer on the fifth day but it was not received by Special Books Ltd until two days later

B   Rose may have a legitiate claim if she posted a letter of acceptance on the third day but, because she used the wrong address, Special Books Ltd did not receive it for another week

C   Special Books Ltd may sell the book immediately to another customer if an acceptance is not received from Rose within the time period specified

D   Special Books Ltd did not specify a method by which Rose should communicate acceptance because specifying a method of acceptance is not allowed by law

(2 marks)

3.6 Sue offered to sell her hamster on 1 May. John received the offer on 2 May. On 4 May he went to see her to accept the offer. He left a letter accepting the offer with her personal assistant. On 3 May, unknown to John, Sue had written to John revoking the offer.

What is the present status of Sue's offer?

A   The offer has been accepted, if the personal assistant is Sue's agent
B   The offer was withdrawn by Sue's letter of revocation
C   The offer will be revoked when John receives the letter from Sue
D   The offer will be accepted when the personal assistant shows Sue John's letter of acceptance   (2 marks)

3.7 **What presumption about the intention to create legal relations does the law make in relation to social and domestic dealings?**

A   It presumes that the parties did intend to create a legally binding contract
B   It presumes that the parties did not intend to create a legally binding contract
C   It does not make any presumptions about the intention of the parties   (1 mark)

3.8 **Which of the following statements relating to contracts with a minor is correct?**

A   A minor can repudiate a contract for necessaries
B   All contracts with minors are unenforceable in the courts
C   Certain types of contract are voidable by a minor
D   Repayment of a loan to a minor is enforceable   (2 marks)

3.9 Felix goes into a shop and sees a price tag for £250 on a compact disc player. He goes to the cash desk to pay for the CD player but is told by the sales assistant that the tag has been wrongly printed and should read £520. Felix maintains that he only has to pay £250.

How should the price on the price tag be regarded in terms of contract law?

A   As an invitation to treat
B   As a tender
C   As an offer
D   As an acceptance   (2 marks)

3.10   On 1 December Donna offered to sell her car to Tim for £1,500 but in reply to her offer he merely asked how many owners it had previously had and whether it had a full service history. Donna provided the information on 2 December and stated that she would leave the offer open until 10 December. On 7 December Tim said he would take the car for £1,250. On 8 December Sophia bought the car from Donna for £1,500. On 10 December, when Tim told Donna he would buy the car for £1,500, he was told that it had been sold.

What is the current state of legal relations between Tim and Donna?

A   There is a contract to sell at £1,250, so Tim may recover the car from Sophia as his property

B   Donna has terminated a contract to sell at £1,500 by having sold the car to Sophia

C   There is an offer from Donna to sell for £1,500 which is still open to Tim to accept

D   There is an offer from Tim to buy at £1,500 which Donna cannot accept   (2 marks)

3.11   **In relation to contract law which of the following statements about an agreement is/are correct?**

(1)   If an agreement is stated to be "binding in honour only", the parties have decided that the agreement is not legally enforceable

(2)   If an agreement is not in writing, the parties are presumed to have intended that it should not be legally enforceable

A   1 only
B   2 only
C   Neither 1 nor 2
D   Both 1 and 2   (2 marks)

3.12   The vast majority of contracts are "simple".
What is the meaning of the word "simple" in this context?

A   The terms of the contract are set out in writing
B   The contract does not need to be in any particular form to be binding
C   The contract is not supported by consideration   (1 mark)

3.13   Charles recently purchased some goods at an auction sale.

Which of the following is correct?

(1)   The contract was concluded by the fall of the Auctioneer's hammer
(2)   The Auctioneer's call for bids was an invitation to treat
(3)   Once the bidding had started, the Auctioneer was unable to withdraw the goods from the sale

A   1 only
B   1 and 2 only
C   2 and 3 only
D   1, 2 and 3   (2 marks)

3.14   **In which of the following is there a presumption that legal relations are intended?**

A   A promise by a father to make a gift to his son
B   A commercial transaction
C   A domestic arrangement   (1 mark)

3.15 On 1 August Daniel sent a letter to Martin offering to sell Martin some steel. On 8 August Daniel sent a further letter revoking the offer. Martin received the original letter of offer on 11 August and immediately posted his letter of acceptance. On 12 August Martin received the letter of revocation.

Is there a contract and why?

A   Yes – Martin has accepted prior to receiving notice of the revocation

B   No – the revocation is effective from the date of posting

C   No – Martin's acceptance is not valid until it reaches Daniel, after Daniel's revocation

D   Yes – revocation of offers cannot be done by post   (2 marks)

3.16 Eric owes Henry £1,000 to be repaid by 30 June next year. At Henry's request Eric pays Henry £800 on 1 December this year in "full satisfaction of the debt".

Can Henry sue Eric for £200 on 30 June?

A   Yes, since part payment of a debt cannot provide satisfaction for the agreement to discharge the debt

B   No, because Henry by his promise will be estopped from insisting on his legal rights

C   Yes, since the payment of £800 on 1 December is not adequate consideration for the promise not to sue

D   No, because part payment early at the request of Henry provides satisfaction for the agreement to discharge the debt   (2 marks)

3.17 **In the context of the law of contract, what is a letter of comfort?**

A   A binding promise

B   A legally-binding guarantee

C   A non-binding letter of intent   (1 mark)

(30 marks)

MCQs 4 CONTRACT LAW – TERMS

4.1 The Consumer Rights Act 2015 deals with exclusion clauses that seek to limit liability.

Which of the following describes such terms that are NOT reasonable?

A   Void

B   Voidable

C   Unenforcable   (1 mark)

4.2 **Additional services performed by an innocent party can be stopped if which of the following is broken under a contract agreement?**

A   Warranty terms

B   Condition terms

C   Innominate terms   (1 mark)

4.3 **Which of the following statements is/are correct?**

(1) A contractual term which attempts to exclude liability for damage to property caused by negligence is void unless it is reasonable

(2) A contractual term which attempts to exclude liability for death or personal injury is void

A 1 only
B 2 only
C Neither 1 nor 2
D Both 1 and 2   (2 marks)

4.4 **Which of the following statements about contract terms is/are correct?**

(1) A condition is a term which the parties intended to be of fundamental importance

(2) A warranty is a term which the parties did not intend to be of fundamental importance

(3) If an innominate term is broken the innocent party has the option whether or not to terminate the contract

A 1 only
B 1 and 2 only
C 2 and 3 only
D 1, 2 and 3   (2 marks)

4.5 **Any ambiguity in the terms of a contract is construed in the favour of which of the following?**

A Consumer
B Seller
C Neither the consumer nor the seller   (1 mark)

4.6 Rose, a hotel proprietor, decides to sell the hotel's microwave cooker and advertises it. Ian, the owner of a bed and breakfast business, inspects the cooker and makes an offer of £100 bearing in mind its general condition. Rose agrees but excludes any liability for "quality and fitness". The cooker refused to work after it was delivered to Ian.

What is the legal position?

A Ian can claim back the £100 since this was a consumer sale in which it is not possible to exclude the condition of satisfactory quality

B Ian aquired the cooker for his own business so this was not a consumer sale and the exclusion clause is valid provided it was reasonable

C Ian cannot claim back the £100 since the price was so low that it is not reasonable for the condition of satisfactory quality to be applied

D Ian can claim back the £100 since an exclusion clause cannot excuse total non-performance of the contract   (2 marks)

4.7 **A contract which lacks some legally required formality is best described as which of the following?**

    A   Unenforceable

    B   Void

    C   Voidable   (1 mark)

4.8 Susan goes to see a play at the theatre. At the box office a notice is displayed which states that the proprietors accept no liability for loss or injury caused, by whatever means, to patrons or their property. On leaving the theatre Susan trips over a poorly-fitted carpet and injures herself. She now wishes to sue the proprietors of the theatre.

What is the validity of the exclusion clause?

    A   It is invalid because it is prohibited by statute

    B   It is invalid because it was not drawn to Susan's attention

    C   It is invalid because it did not constitute a term of the contract

    D   It is valid and Susan's claim will fail   (2 marks)

4.9 **Breach of which of the following terms does NOT permit the innocent party to repudiate a contract?**

    A   A condition

    B   An innominate term

    C   A warranty   (1 mark)

4.10 **In the context of contract law, which of the following statements about a condition in a contract is true?**

    A   It is a minor term, breach of which entitles the innocent party to claim damages

    B   It is a term, breach of which entitles the innocent party to repudiate the contract if the effects of the breach are serious

    C   It is a major term, breach of which entitles the innocent party to repudiate the contract if he wishes and/or claim damages   (1 mark)

4.11 **A term will NOT be implied into a contract by which of the following?**

    A   By statute

    B   By a court because it is customary

    C   By a court to make the contract more equitable

    D   By a court on the ground of business efficacy   (2 marks)

4.12 **Which of the following statements about contract terms is NOT correct?**

    A   A condition is intended to be of fundamental importance

    B   A warranty is not intended to be of fundamental importance

    C   If a condition is breached the contract must be terminated

    D   If a warranty is breached the innocent party cannot terminate the contract (2 marks)

4.13 DE Ltd contracted to deliver a quantity of goods to F Ltd to the value of £5,000. The goods were delivered and DE Ltd submitted an invoice to F Ltd for the amount due which contained a number of new terms.

Which of the following statements is NOT correct?

A   The invoice is a contractual document and F Ltd is bound by the terms on the invoice

B   F Ltd is only bound by the terms if it was given notice of them at or before the time of contract

C   F Ltd is only bound by the terms if there has been a sufficient course of dealings between DE Ltd and F Ltd so that F Ltd is assumed to know of the terms

D   If F Ltd is unaware of the terms, it can only be bound by them if it agrees to be so

(2 marks)

4.14   A enters into a partnership agreement with B, a minor.

Which of the following describes the agreement?

A   It is void
B   It is voidable by B only
C   It is voidable by A only
D   It is voidable by both A and B   (2 marks)

4.15   **Which of the following describes a contract that is entered into as a result of the coercion of one party by the other?**

A   Unenforceable
B   Valid
C   Void   (1 mark)

4.16   **In relation to contractual terms, which of the following is the consequence of a term having more than one meaning?**

A   The term is assumed to be not binding
B   The interpretation most favourable to the consumer prevails
C   The term is not binding on the consumer unless he chooses to be bound by it

(1 mark)

4.17   **Under the Consumer Rights Act 2015 all products must meet which of the following standards?**

(1)   Satisfactory quality
(2)   Fit for purpose
(3)   As described

A   1 only
B   1 and 2 only
C   1 and 3 only
D   1, 2 and 3   (2 marks)

4.18   In general, terms used in contracts and notices will only be binding upon the consumer if they are fair.

To which of the following does the "fairness test" apply to terms in a consumer contract?

A   All terms
B   Only exclusion terms
C   All terms except the price payable
D   Any term that is not sufficiently transparent or prominent   (2 marks)

(28 marks)

MCQs 5 CONTRACT LAW – BREACH

5.1   ABC Ltd has contracted with DEF Ltd.

If ABC Ltd acts in breach of a warranty, which of the following actions may DEF Ltd take?

(1)   DEF Ltd may terminate the contract and sue for damages
(2)   DEF Ltd may sue for damages but may not terminate the contract
(3)   DEF Ltd may ignore the breach and continue with the contract

A   1 only
B   1 and 3 only
C   2 and 3 only
D   1, 2 and 3   (2 marks)

5.2   Den, a publican, orders 12 crates of stout with 12 half litre bottles per crate. The correct number of bottles are delivered but in six crates of 24 half litre bottles per crate. Den rejects the delivery of the whole consignment.

What is Den's liability in contract law?

A   There is no breach of condition or warranty as this is not a consumer sale, therefore Den is liable for breach of contract

B   There has only been a breach of warranty, therefore Den must pay and claim damages

C   Den is in breach of contract by rejecting the goods and is liable to pay damages

D   There has been a breach of condition that the goods match the description, therefore Den is entitled to treat the contract as discharged   (2 marks)

5.3   **What does a breach of a condition entitle the injured party to do?**

A   Claim damages only
B   Sue on a *quantum meruit*
C   Repudiate the contract and claim damages   (1 mark)

5.4   **Which of the following contracts could be enforceable by an order of specific performance?**

A   A contract with a minor
B   A contract of employment
C   A contract for the loan of money
D   A contract for the purchase of land   (2 marks)

5.5 Following a written private order for 50 cases of brown ale, with 12 one pint bottles per case, Mr Ramsbottom finds that he has been sent the equivalent order in larger one litre bottles. His rejection of the entire consignment incurs additional cost to the supplier who commences legal action for breach of contract.

What is Mr Ramsbottom's liability in contract law?

A He is liable for breach of contract as repudiation is not possible the supplier's breach of warranty

B He is not liable as he was entitled to repudiate the contract for the breach of the condition that the goods must match the description

C He is not liable as his purchase was not a consumer sale

D He is liable for breach of contract as any packaging of goods is only a warranty and he did not have the right to repudiate it (2 marks)

5.6 **To what extent are damages awarded for a breach of contract?**

A To put the innocent party in the position he would have been in if the contract had been performed

B To restore the position of the innocent party to what it would have been if the contract had never been made

C To put the innocent party in the position he would have been in had the contract been performed plus an amount of compensation

D To restore the position of the innocent to what it would have been if the contract had never been made plus an amount of compensation (2 marks)

5.7 **What does a claimant's duty to mitigate his losses mean?**

A The claimant must take reasonable steps to ensure that his damages are kept to a minimum

B The claimant must produce an itemised list of damages with supporting evidence otherwise he will not be able to recover losses

C The claimant cannot claim for losses that occur after the court hearing so he must not expect to be compensated for future losses

D The claimant must deduct the cost of his legal expenses from his claim for damages as each party must pay his own legal bills in a civil claim (2 marks)

5.8 **Which of the following contracts might be specifically enforceable?**

A Alan has contracted to sell his house to Bob but has changed his mind and no longer wishes to sell it

B Chris has contracted to buy a new Ford motor car but the garage is now refusing to honour the contract

C Diane has contracted to purchase a number of tins of fruit for her business, but the seller has now stated that he no longer wishes to proceed with the contract

D Eduardo has contracted to sing at a concert organised by Fernando, but Eduardo has withdrawn as he has received a more lucrative offer from Giovanni (2 marks)

5.9 **In the event of a breach of contract, what is the purpose of damages?**

    (1)   To punish the party in breach of the contract
    (2)   To compensate the innocent party
    (3)   To put the innocent party in the same position as if the contract had been carried out correctly

    A   1 and 2 only
    B   2 and 3 only
    C   1 and 3 only
    D   1, 2 and 3   (2 marks)

5.10 **Which of the following remedies for breach of contract must be awarded by the court if there has been a breach of contract?**

    A   An injunction
    B   Damages
    C   Specific performance   (1 mark)

5.11 **Which of the following statements relating to a liquidated damages clause are correct?**

    (1)   It will be void if it amounts to a penalty clause
    (2)   It will be valid if it is a genuine estimate of the likely loss foreseeable
    (3)   It cannot be valid if it is for an amount that exceeds the actual loss caused by the breach of contract

    A   1 and 2 only
    B   1 and 3 only
    C   2 and 3 only
    D   1, 2 and 3   (2 marks)

5.12 **Which of the following entitles the innocent party to cancel the contract?**

    (1)   A breach of a warranty
    (2)   A breach of a condition
    (3)   An express term authorising termination of the contract

    A   1 only
    B   1 and 2 only
    C   2 and 3 only
    D   1, 2 and 3   (2 marks)

5.13 **What is the equitable remedy of rescission?**

    A   An order that the parties terminate their actions under the contract
    B   An order that forces the parties to respect their contractual obligations
    C   A payment award to the parties for any reasonable acts they have undertaken
    D   An order that the parties be placed in their exact pre-contractual positions

               (2 marks)

5.14 One party to a contract announces, before the time for performance, that he does not intend to perform his obligations on the due date.

What is the term for this in contract law?

    A   Affirmation
    B   Anticipatory breach
    C   Fundamental breach   (1 mark)

5.15 Colin agreed to build a summer house for Terry at a price of £4,000. When he had completed the foundations he had an argument with Terry's wife and, in a fit of anger, abandoned the job. He sends Terry a bill for £1,500, which is less than the cost of the work he has done. Terry refuses to pay.

What grounds does Colin have for seeking payment from Terry?

A   In equity it is fair that Terry pays the £1,500 as it is less than the cost of the work done

B   Colin has no grounds as he has not performed the contract and is not entitled to compensation since he abandoned it

C   In equity Colin is entitled to a payment quantum merit for the value of the work done

D   As due to an unforeseen circumstance Colin cannot complete the contract he may sue Terry for a reasonable price for the work done   (2 marks)

5.16 Keith engaged Krafty Kitchens Ltd to install a new fitted kitchen in his home for £10,000. On completion of the work Keith discovered that one of the electrical appliances was not wired properly and the work surfaces were incorrectly fitted. Keith engaged a local electrician and carpenter to remedy the defects at a cost of £1,000. Krafty Kitchens Ltd is now pressing for payment of £10,000.

What is the legal position?

A   Keith is liable to pay the full £10,000 as the contract is complete

B   Keith is liable to pay £9,000 (i.e. the contract price less the cost of repairs) as substantial performance has occurred

C   Keith is not liable to pay anything to Krafty Kitchens Ltd as it has not substantially performed the contract and is in fact in breach of contract

D   Keith is liable to pay a reasonable sum only, which must be assessed by the court   (2 marks)

5.17 **Where there has been an anticipatory breach of contract, when is the earliest point at which the injured party is entitled to sue?**

A   After a reasonable time has elapsed
B   At the point when the other party indicates that he is not prepared to be bound
C   At the point when the other party actually fails to perform a contractual condition
D   When the injured party has completely fulfilled his obligations, but the other party indicates that he does not intend to be bound   (2 marks)

5.18 Askey agreed to build a supermarket complex for Hancock to be completed on 1 December. The contract provided for a penalty of £1,000 per day from 1 December to date of actual completion.

The building was 20 days late and as a result Hancock was able to prove that he had lost £200,000 of revenue and £50,000 of profits in the Christmas shopping period.

What is the maximum amount he may recover from Askey?

A   Nil
B   £20,000
C   £50,000
D   £200,000   (2 marks)

5.19   Rose ordered a new Skoda Octavia estate car from her local Skoda car dealer. The price was agreed at £17,000 and Rose signed an order form. Subsequently she changed her mind and refused to take delivery. The dealers sold the car to Sara for £16,300 but sued Rose for not taking delivery.

In contract law, what is Rose's liability?

A   Rose is liable to the dealer for the loss of the profit it would have made on the sale to Rose

B   Rose is not liable since the dealer has sold the car to Sara

C   Rose is liable to the dealer for £700, being the reduction in the price to Sara

D   Rose is not liable as the dealer should have mitigated the loss and sold the car to someone other than Sara for £17,000   (2 marks)

5.20   **What is the time limit for a claim for damages for breach of a simple contract where there is no personal injury claim?**

A   Within two years of the time the cause of action arose
B   Within six years of the time the cause of action arose
C   Within twelve years of the time the cause of action arose   (1 mark)

5.21   The directors of Wimpish Construction discover a clause in a road-building contract for the Bassetshire County Council whereby they will be liable to "the sum of £1,000 per day" if they are late with completion of the contract.

Can this clause be enforced against Wimpish?

A   No, penalty clauses will never be enforced by the courts
B   Yes, provided it is a custom of the trade
C   No, penalty clauses are an attempt to punish, not compensate
D   Yes, provided the sum is a genuine estimate of the likely loss where precise quantification is difficult   (2 marks)

5.22   Better Builders Ltd contracted to build a new showroom for Magic Motors Ltd. The contract provided that Better Builders would pay Magic Motors £1,000 per week if completion were to be delayed.

There was a delay of 17 weeks. Magic Motors sued for £58,000, being £40,000 normal trading profits which were lost and £18,000 relating to a special contract to hold a motor fair on behalf of Park Lane Cars plc.

What level of damages will Magic Motors be able to claim?

A   £17,000
B   £18,000
C   £40,000
D   £58,000   (2 marks)

(40 marks)

MCQs 6 EMPLOYMENT LAW

6.1 **Which TWO of the following are tests applied by the courts to distinguish an employee from an independent contractor?**

(1)   Officious bystander test
(2)   Control test
(3)   Economic reality test
(4)   Fit and proper test

A   1 and 2
B   1 and 4
C   2 and 3
D   3 and 4   (2 marks)

6.2 **Which of the following is NOT a common law duty of care of employers towards employees?**

A   Duty to provide safe premises
B   Duty to provide competent staff
C   Duty to provide a safe system of work
D   Duty to provide rest periods and breaks   (2 marks)

6.3 **Which of the following statements suggests that John is an independent contractor in relation to the work he carries out for Zed Ltd?**

(1)   He is required to provide his own tools
(2)   He is required to carry out his work personally and is not free to send a substitute
(3)   He is paid a gross rate without any deduction of income tax

A   1 and 2 only
B   2 and 3 only
C   1 and 3 only
D   1, 2 and 3   (2 marks)

6.4 **Which of the following is normally implied into a contract of employment?**

A   The employer's duty to provide a reference
B   The employer's duty to provide work
C   The employer's duty to pay wages   (1 mark)

6.5 An employer dismisses three employees on the following grounds:

(1)   Andre, for his involvement in trade union activities
(2)   Bertha, for having become pregnant
(3)   Colin, for refusing to obey a reasonable instruction

Who has a valid claim for unfair dismissal

A   Andre and Bertha only
B   Bertha and Colin only
C   Andre and Colin only
D   Andre, Bertha and Colin   (2 marks)

6.6   **Which of the following is NOT a duty of an employer?**

  A   To provide an employee with a reference when he leaves employment

  B   To allow Health and Safety representatives reasonable paid time off work to perform their functions

  C   To provide appropriate training   (1 mark)

6.7   An employer agrees to provide a new employee with a written statement of particulars of his employment.

  When must this be given to the employee?

  A   Immediately on commencement of the employment
  B   Within one month of the employment commencing
  C   Within two months of the employment commencing
  D   Within three months of the employment commencing   (2 marks)

6.8   **Which of the following statements about employer's obligations is correct?**

  A   An employer with fewer than 20 employees is not obliged to comply with national minimum wage requirements

  B   An employer is obliged to give only one week's notice of termination to employees with one year of service

  C   An employer is obliged to provide employees with a designated smoking area for use in authorised rest periods and breaks

  D   Only employers with more than 20 employees are obliged to provide employees with a detailed pay slip   (2 marks)

6.9   **Which of the following statements about dismissal is correct?**

  A   A wrongful dismissal cannot also be an unfair dismissal
  B   An unfair dismissal can also be a wrongful dismissal
  C   An unfair dismissal must also be a wrongful dismissal   (1 mark)

6.10   Brian has been employed by Wye Ltd for 10 years. His contract of employment states that if either Wye Ltd or Brian wishes to terminate the contract, each party must give the statutory minimum period of notice.

  How much notice must Brian and Wye give to each other?

	Brian to Wye Ltd	*Wye Ltd to Brian*
A	One week	One week
B	One week	Ten weeks
C	Ten weeks	One week
D	Ten weeks	Ten weeks (2 marks)

6.11   **Which of the following remedies is NOT available for claims of unfair dismissal?**

  A   Compensation
  B   Re-instatement
  C   Re-engagement
  D   Specific performance   (2 marks)

6.12   Bernard's employment as a part-time store manager with Exe Ltd commenced three years ago. Following a meeting with other employees of Exe Ltd, it was agreed that Bernard be appointed Health and Safety Representative. Bernard agreed that as part of this role he would insist on having monthly meetings with the management of Exe Ltd. Exe Ltd considered this to be excessive and dismissed Bernard giving him one week's notice.

What is Bernard' legal position?

A   He cannot claim unfair dismissal because he does not have the relevant period of continuous employment

B   He cannot claim unfair dismissal because he is a part-time worker

C   He can claim unfair dismissal

D   He can claim wrongful dismissal   (2 marks)

6.13   **Which of the following statements about the vicarious liability of an employer is/are correct?**

(1)   An employer is vicariously liable for the torts of employees committed in the course of their employment

(2)   An employer is vicariously liable for the torts of independent contractors, if they were committed whilst carrying out work for the employer

A   1 only
B   2 only
C   Both 1 and 2
D   Neither 1 nor 2   (2 marks)

6.14   **In relation to a claim for wrongful dismissal, which of the following statements is correct?**

(1)   Only employees below the normal retiring age may claim
(2)   There is no limit on the amount of compensation that a tribunal can award
(3)   Claims must be made within three months of the dismissal

A   1 only
B   2 only
C   3 only
D   Neither 1, 2 nor 3   (2 marks)

6.15   **In the tests applied by the Courts to determine an employment relationship, which test considers how the individual is paid?**

A   Control test
B   Integration test
C   Economic reality test   (1 mark)

6.16   A part-time worker wishes to claim for unfair dismissal.

For how many years must he have been continuously employed before the effective date of termination?

A   One year
B   Two years
C   Three years   (1 mark)

6.17 The Enterprise and Regulatory Reform Act 2013 sets out the use of a settlement agreement to resolve employment disputes.

Which TWO of the following statements about a settlement agreement are correct?

(1) It is mandatory
(2) It must be in writing
(3) It may be proposed by an employee
(4) It must be made at the beginning of an employment relationship

A 1 and 2
B 1 and 4
C 2 and 3
D 3 and 4   (2 marks)

6.18 Phil has agreed to perform work for a company conditionally on the company making work available to him.

Which of the following describes a term which prohibits Phil from working for someone else without the company's consent?

A Legitimate
B Unenforceable
C Voidable
D Valid   (2 marks)

(31 marks)

MCQs 7 AGENCY

7.1 **Which of the following conditions is necessary in order for a principal to be able to ratify a contract entered into by an agent?**

A The principal need only have contractual capacity when the contract is ratified
B The principal need only have contractual capacity when the contract was entered into
C The agent must have contractual capacity when the contract was entered into
D The principal must have contractual capacity when the contract was entered into and when it is ratified   (2 marks)

7.2 Barry is managing director of Soap Ltd. He enters into a contract to buy some property on behalf of the company.

What is the legal position?

A The contract is invalid and must be ratified by the members
B The contract is valid as Barry has implied authority to act in this way
C The contract is invalid as Barry has not acted out of necessity
D The contract is invalid as the contract must be by deed   (2 marks)

7.3 Benskin retired from the firm of Cropper & Co in 20X2 yet still wanted to be involved in some capacity. Cropper & Co continued to allow Benskin to negotiate contracts even though he had no appointed authority to enter into contracts on behalf of the company.

On what basis could Cropper & Co be liable as a principal for contracts made in 20X3 on behalf of Cropper & Co by Benskin?

A	By agency of necessity
B	By ratification by implication
C	Only if he expressly authorises them
D	By apparent authority (by estoppel)	(2 marks)

7.4 Arthur entered into a contract with Ted without disclosing that he was acting as an agent on the instructions of Patricia.

What right does Ted have?

A Ted may sue Arthur only, as he had no knowledge that he was an agent

B Ted may sue Patricia only, because Arthur was in fact an agent

C Ted may sue Patricia or Arthur, since Arthur was acting as an agent for an undisclosed principal

D Ted may sue Patricia and Arthur, since Patricia and Arthur are treated as principals

(2 marks)

7.5 William, an adult, appointed Chelsea, who is aged 16, to act as his agent in running his business. Chelsea appoints Hillary, who is 20, to act on her behalf in the acquisition of some non-essential items.

Which agent(s) has/have been validly appointed?

A	Chelsea only
B	Hillary only
C	Both Chelsea and Hillary
D	Neither Chelsea nor Hillary	(2 marks)

7.6 A principal refuses to ratify a contract entered into by an agent in his own name on the principal's behalf but in excess of that agent's authority.

Who may the third party concerned sue?

A	The principal only
B	The agent or the principal
C	The agent only
D	The agent and the principal	(2 marks)

7.7 **Which of the following events does NOT necessarily terminate agency?**

A	The death of the principal
B	The death of the agent
C	The bankruptcy of the agent	(1 mark)

7.8 **Which of the following statements regarding ratification of contracts by the principal is NOT correct?**

A	The principal must tell the third party the agent is acting for him
B	The principal must ratify the contract within a reasonable time
C	The principal must have the capacity to contract	(1 mark)

7.9 Alex instructed Patricia, his agent, to place a bet on a horse in a race, at a time when gambling had been declared illegal. The horse won but Patricia had not placed the bet.

Can Alex recover the potential winnings from Patricia and why?

A Yes, because Patricia did not obey his instruction
B Yes, because Patricia has a duty to render accounts to the principal whenever required
C No, because Patricia acted in good faith
D No, because Alex's instruction was not lawful (2 marks)

7.10 Colin appointed Miles, an estate agent, as sole agent for the sale of his house. The agreed rate of commission was 2%. Miles passed the details to another estate agent, Simon, who sent his own client, Alec, to view it. Colin and Alec agreed a sale.

What commission can Miles claim from Colin on the successful completion of the sale?

A The full commission, as a buyer has been found and the flat has been sold successfully

B No commission, since Miles has not personally carried out the duties entrusted to him

C No ommission, since Miles has not exercised due skill and care in the performance of his duties

D The full commission, since it was reasonable for Miles to delegate to another estate agent in this situation and it enabled a buyer to be found (2 marks)

7.11 A transport company was contracted to move the musical equipment for a group of musicians. When the company arrived at the location of the concert, the building was locked and nobody was there to receive the equipment. The company made a decision to store the musical equipment in a storage facility overnight.

Which of the following describes the authority of the company to store the musical equipment?

A Express authority of an agent
B Implied authority
C Apparent authority
D Agency by necessity (2 marks)

7.12 By virtue of his position as managing director of a company a person has implied authority to bind the company by his acts.

Which of the following represents the full limit of this authority?

A All commercial matters relating to the running of the business
B All activities of the company whether commercial or not
C Such commercial activities as are delegated to him by the board of directors
D Such commercial activities as are directed by the company in general meeting (2 marks)

7.13 What is ostensible authority?

A Actual authority
B Apparent authority
C Implied actual authority (1 mark)

7.14   Even in cases where there are no express words, authority may still arise through
_____.

Which words complete correctly complete this sentence?

A   Agreement by conduct
B   Implied actual authority
C   Authorised authority
D   Unspoken agreement   (2 marks)

7.15   **When does apparent authority arise?**

A   When the agent implies that he has authority
B   When the principal and the third party make a contract
C   When the principal represents to a third party that the agent has authority

(1 mark)

(26 marks)

MCQs 8 PARTNERSHIP

8.1   Adam, Ben and Carol have carried on business together in partnership since July. In September they decided to enter into a formal partnership agreement. The partners agreed the terms of the agreement in October and signed the completed agreement in November.

When did the partnership commence?

A   July
B   September
C   October
D   November   (2 marks)

8.2   **Which of the following statements regarding partnerships is correct?**

A   A limited partner may lose his limited liability if he begins to be more actively involved in the day-to-day business of a limited liability partnership

B   An incoming partner immediately becomes liable for all debts incurred before his admission

C   The estate of a deceased partner is not liable for debts incurred before the partner's death   (1 mark)

8.3   Partners in trading firms have implied authority:

(1)   To receive payment of debts due to the firm
(2)   To borrow money on the firm's credit
(3)   To sell goods belonging to the firm
(4)   To engage employees for the business

What are implied authorities of partners of non-trading firms?

A   1, 2 and 3
B   1, 2 and 4
C   1, 3 and 4
D   2, 3 and 4   (2 marks)

8.4   **What is the liability of partners for the tortious acts of each other carried out in the normal course of business?**

    A   Joint
    B   Several
    C   Joint or several
    D   Joint and several   (2 marks)

8.5   **For which of the following does a partner have no apparent authority, regardless of the nature of the firm?**

    A   Receive payments of debts due and give receipts
    B   Secure a loan to the firm by depositing title deeds with the lender
    C   Employ a solicitor to defend the firm in a legal action
    D   Compromise a debt by receiving something other than money in settlement
                                                                                                                                            (2 marks)

8.6   A partner who retires from his firm is required to place an advertisement to that effect in the *London Gazette*.

    To whom is this advertisement deemed to give notice?

    A   Anyone who reads the advertisement

    B   Anyone, whether they read the advertisement or not, who had not previously dealt with the firm but who knew the person to be a partner

    C   Anyone who reads the advertisement who had not previously dealt with the firm but who knew the individual to be a partner

    D   Anyone, whether they read the advertisement or not, and regardless of their previous relationship with the firm   (2 marks)

8.7   **Which of the following statements in relation to partnership law is NOT correct?**

    A   In England, a partnership has no existence separate from the partners
    B   Each partner can bind the firm in contract if acting in the ordinary course of business
    C   Partners are never liable for debts contracted before they became partners
    D   To be binding, a partnership agreement must be in writing   (2 marks)

8.8   **On which of the following grounds is a court order needed for dissolution of a partnership on application by a partner?**

    A   On the expiration of the fixed term for which the partnership was created
    B   On bankruptcy or death of a partner
    C   On a charging order being made against a partner
    D   On the permanent incapacity of a partner   (2 marks)

8.9   **What is a partnership according to the Partnership Act 1890?**

    A   A relation which subsist between two people carrying on a business in common with a view to profit

    B   A relation which subsists between persons carrying on a business in common with a view to profit or loss

    C   A relation which subsists between persons carrying on a business in common with a view to profit   (1 mark)

8.10 A restaurant is owned by a partnership whose partners are Ted, Lauren, and Richard. Lauren and Richard are actively involved in the business and run the restaurant on a daily basis. Ted initially contributed money to form the partnership and shares in profits of the business but does not participate in the operations of the restaurant.

Ted can be described as which of the following types of partners?

A   General partner
B   Fixed share partner
C   Sleeping partner
D   Nominal partner   (2 marks)

8.11 Dennis was a partner in Doolittle Solicitors. He retired from the partnership and the firm's existing clients were informed of this fact and the firm amended its stationery so that Dennis's name no longer appeared on it. Subsequently, Dennis, using old stationery on which his name is printed, ordered goods and asked for the invoice to be sent to Doolittle Solicitors.

Which of the following statements is correct?

A   There is a binding contract between Dennis and the supplier of the goods

B   No binding contract has been created between the supplier and Doolittle Solicitors because Dennis was not authorised to act on behalf of the firm

C   There is a binding contract between Doolittle Solicitors and the supplier of the goods

D   No binding contract has been created because the partnership shown on the stationery had ceased to exist   (2 marks)

8.12 **Which of the following are statutory rights of a partner under the Partnership Act 1890?**

(1)   To share in the capital, profits and losses of the business in proportion to their initial capital contribution to the firm

(2)   To have unfettered access to the firm's books and accounts

A   1 only
B   2 only
C   Neither 1 nor 2
D   Both 1 and 2   (2 marks)

8.13 Under the Limited Liability Partnerships Act 2000 certain requirements need to be met for a limited liability partnership (LLP) to be legitimately formed.

Which of the following are among those requirements?

(1)   One or more persons who are associated for the purposes of carrying on a lawful business with a view to a profit must have subscribed their names to an incorporation document

(2)   The incorporation document must state the name of the LLP which must end with the words "Limited Liability Partnership" or the abbreviation "LLP"

A   1 only
B   2 only
C   Neither 1 nor 2
D   Both 1 and 2   (2 marks)

8.14   **In the absence of any agreement to the contrary, the rights of members of a limited liability partnership include which of the following?**

    (1)   An equal share in the capital and profits of the limited liability partnership
    (2)   Remuneration for acting in the business or management of the limited liability partnership

    A   1 only
    B   2 only
    C   Neither 1 nor 2
    D   Both 1 and 2   (2 marks)

8.15   Peter and Paul are partners in the Connaught Quick-Repair Garage. Under the terms of the partnership agreement, trading in motor vehicles is prohibited. While Peter was on holiday, Paul, purporting to act on behalf of the partnership, sold a car. The car is completely un-roadworthy and the purchaser sues Peter and Paul under the Consumer Rights Act 2015.

   What is Peter's liability to the customer?

    A   Peter is not liable as Paul was not authorised to sell cars

    B   Peter is liable since the sale of the car was the kind of transaction a garage business might undertake

    C   The purchaser can take action against Peter or Paul

    D   Peter is not liable unless he subsequently ratified the sale   (2 marks)

                                                                     (28 marks)

MCQs 9 CORPORATIONS AND LEGAL PERSONALITY

9.1   **In relation to company law, which of the following statements is correct?**

    A   A company limited by shares is fully liable for all its debts
    B   Shareholders are fully liable for the debts of the company
    C   Directors are fully liable for the debts of the company   (1 mark)

9.2   Quentin was employed by Bee Ltd as its senior design consultant. Quentin contracted with Bee Ltd that when his employment with the company ceased, he would not act in competition with it or solicit its customers. After Quentin left Bee Ltd, he registered a company called Cee Ltd, which immediately began working in competition with Bee Ltd and soliciting its customers.

   Which of the following is correct?

    A   Quentin is not in breach of the agreement with Bee Ltd because Cee Ltd is a separate legal entity

    B   Since Cee Ltd was formed to avoid the non-compete agreement the courts will "lift the corporate veil" and enforce the agreement

    C   Cee Ltd will be bound by the agreement because a company is always liable for the actions of its shareholders.

    D   The non-compete agreement has no legal effect as it attempts to regulate Quentin's activities after he has left Bee Ltd's employment   (2 marks)

9.3 **Which of the following statements about companies is correct?**

A   The shares of all public limited companies are quoted on the Stock Exchange

B   The company secretary of a public limited company must be qualified by examination or experience

C   A private limited company must have at least two shareholders   (1 mark)

9.4 **Which of the following statements about a company limited by shares are correct?**

(1)   A company is owned by its shareholders and managed by its directors

(2)   A company is entitled to own property in its own name

(3)   The shareholders can never incur personal liability over and above the amount due on their shares even if the veil of incorporation is lifted

A   1 and 2 only
B   1 and 3 only
C   2 and 3 only
D   1, 2 and 3   (2 marks)

9.5 **Which of the following is a consequence of corporate personality?**

(1)   The company is fully liable for its own debts
(2)   A shareholder has limited liability
(3)   If a wrong is done to the company, the general rule is that only the company is entitled to sue

A   1 and 2 only
B   1 and 3 only
C   2 and 3 only
D   1, 2 and 3   (2 marks)

9.6 **Which of the following statements are correct in relation to companies limited by shares?**

(1)   A private company must have at least one director
(2)   A public company must have at least two directors
(3)   A private company must have authorised share capital of at least £30,000
(4)   A public company must have issued share capital of at least £50,000

A   1, 2 and 3
B   1, 2 and 4
C   1, 3 and 4
D   2, 3 and 4   (2 marks)

9.7 **What is the basis for the rule in *Foss v Harbottle*?**

A   The separate legal personality of a company
B   The limited liability of members of a company
C   The common law right of a minority not to be prejudiced   (1 mark)

9.8 **Which of the following statements about a company is NOT true?**

A   A company is a legal person
B   The shares of a public limited company must be quoted on the stock exchange
C   It is possible for a company to be convicted of a criminal offence   (1 mark)

9.9 Mark incorporates his own manufacturing business, King Kilts, under the name King Kilts Ltd. He lent King Kilts Ltd £20,000 and owns 95% of its shares. He continued to insure the company's assets, including the factory, in his own name, as he had always done prior to incorporation. On New Year's Eve, the factory was destroyed by fire.

Can Mark claim on the insurance and for what reason?

A   Yes, because King Kilts Ltd is essentially no different from the original business

B   Yes, because he has an insurable interest as a creditor of King Kilts Ltd

C   Yes, because he has an insurable interest as a member of King Kilts Ltd

D   No, because the insurance is not in the name of King Kilts Ltd and the company has the insurable interest   (2 marks)

9.10 The following data relates to two companies, Steve Ltd and Howe Ltd, for the year ended 30 June 2017:

	Average staff headcount	Net turnover	Balance sheet total
Steve Ltd	9	£1 million	£250,000
Howe Ltd	8	£600,000	£300,000

Which company may be defined as a micro company in accordance with the Small Business, Enterprise and Employment Act 2015?

A   Steve Ltd only
B   How Ltd only
C   Neither Steve Ltd nor How Ltd
D   Both Steve Ltd and How Ltd   (2 marks)

(16 marks)

MCQs 10 FORMATION OF A COMPANY

10.1 A business has been registered under the name "The Mark Jones Partnership Co Ltd".

What type of business organisation must this be?

A   A partnership
B   A private limited company
C   A public limited company
D   Any of the above as this is a business name   (2 marks)

10.2 **Which of the following statements about company formation are correct?**

(1) Purchasing a company "off the shelf" enables business to commence more quickly

(2) It is generally cheaper to purchase a company "off the shelf" than to arrange for a solicitor or accountant to register a new company

(3) Incorporating a company by registration enables the company's documents to be drafted to the particular needs of the incorporators

A   1 and 2 only
B   2 and 3 only
C   1 and 3 only
D   1, 2 and 3   (2 marks)

10.3 **Which of the following statements about a company limited by shares is correct?**

(1) It is not possible to register a company limited by shares with the same name as a company already on the register

(2) Once on the register, a company limited by shares cannot change its registered office

A   1 only
B   2 only
C   Both 1 and 2
D   Neither 1 nor 2   (2 marks)

10.4 **Which of the following statements relating to the commencement of trade by a company are correct?**

(1) A public company cannot commence trading until it has received a trading certificate from the Registrar of Companies

(2) If a public company commences trading without a trading certificate, the directors may be held jointly and severally liable for obligations arising

(3) A private company may commence trading upon receipt of its certificate of incorporation

A   1 and 2 only
B   2 and 3 only
C   1 and 3 only
D   1, 2 and 3   (2 marks)

10.5 **Which of the following statements about the formation of a company is NOT correct?**

A   Promoters must include a Memorandum of Association in the documents submitted to the Registrar of Companies

B   A company cannot be registered with the same number as a company already on the register

C   A company must include a statement of authorised capital in its articles of association

D   The directors of a newly-registered company cannot also act as directors of another company   (2 marks)

10.6 Frederick was the promoter of a limited company to be called Duke's Wines Ltd. The company was incorporated on 1 February 2016. In December 2015 Frederick bought wine to the value of £2,000 from Oliver and signed the contract "Frederick, as agent for Duke's Wines Ltd". On 1 February Duke's Wines Ltd ratified the contract made by Frederick and on 1 March 2016 went into liquidation without having paid Oliver.

Who is liable to Oliver for the debt?

A Duke's Wines Ltd alone, as principal, since the contract was entered into by Frederick as agent for the company

B Duke's Wines Ltd alone since it ratified the contract made on its behalf by Frederick

C Frederick is jointly liable with Duke's Wines Ltd since he was not an agent when he entered into the contract

D Frederick only since ratification by the company was not possible (2 marks)

10.7 The main object of a company is to contract refuse collection services for Westminster City Council.

Which of the following names would NOT be permissible name under the *Companies Act* 2006 without further consent?

A Westminster City Refuse Services Ltd
B Council (Refuse Collection) Services Ltd
C Refuse Collection (Westminster) Ltd
D City Waste Disposal Ltd (2 marks)

10.8 **Who of the following is NOT a member of a company?**

A A person who subscribes to the memorandum of association but whose name has not been entered in the register of members

B A person who has been allocated shares and entered on the register of members but who has not received notification of this

C A person who has lodged a share transfer with the company but who has not been entered on the register of members (1 mark)

10.9 On 1 January Jhalman signed a contract for the supply of trousers to Tasteful Clothes Ltd, which was incorporated on 2 February.

If the trousers are not paid for, who is liable?

A The company, as the contract was signed on its behalf by its agent

B Jhalman and the company are jointly liable, as Jhalman exceeded his authority as agent for the company

C Jhalman, as he was acting on behalf of a principal that did not exist

D The company, provided it ratified the contract after incorporation (2 marks)

10.10 **Which of the following statements about different types of companies are correct?**

(1) A public limited company may commence trading as soon as it receives a certificate of incorporation

(2) A private company may re-register as a public company by passing a special resolution

(3) An unlimited company cannot re-register as a limited company

A 1 only
B 2 only
C 1 and 3 only
D 2 and 3 only (2 marks)

10.11 **To whom must the memorandum of association and articles be delivered to in order to achieve incorporation of a company?**

A The Office of Company Registration
B Company Registration Ltd
C The company's registered office
D Registrar of Companies (2 marks)

10.12 **Which of the following statements relating to a company promoter are true?**

(1) A promoter does not have legal liability for pre-incorporation contracts

(2) A company can claim damages from a promoter who took a secret profit when promoting the company

(3) A promoter is in a fiduciary position for the company he promotes

A 1 only
B 2 only
C 1 and 3 only
D 2 and 3 only (2 marks)

10.13 **Which of the following statements relating to *ultra vires* transactions is correct?**

A A company can enter into any transaction as the doctrine of *ultra vires* has been abolished

B The directors may ratify any *ultra vires* transaction

C A third party who has acted in good faith may enforce an *ultra vires* transaction against the company (1 mark)

10.14 **Which of the following relating to *ultra vires* is NOT correct?**

A If a company's object is to carry on business as a "general commercial company", the company may carry on any trade or business whatsoever

B If a company acts outside its objects clause, it has acted *ultra vires* and the transaction is void

C A company may ratify an *ultra vires* act by passing a special resolution (1 mark)

10.15   A company's statutory books are usually kept at the company's registered office.

Which of the following is a shareholder legally entitled to inspect?

A   The company's books of account
B   Minutes of board meetings
C   The register of charges   (1 mark)

10.16   Which of the following are persons with significant control?

(1)   Gradman Ltd, which owns 55% of the shares of Geraci Ltd
(2)   Beth, who holds 30% of the voting rights of Meginley Ltd
(3)   Ben, who owns 20% of the shares of Light Ltd

A   1 only
B   2 only
C   1 and 2
D   2 and 3   (2 marks)

(28 marks)

MCQs 11 MEMORANDUM AND ARTICLES

11.1   A private company wishes to alter its articles of association.

What resolution must be passed by the shareholders?

A   A special resolution
B   An ordinary resolution
C   An extraordinary resolution   (1 mark)

11.2   Which of the following statements relating to articles of association is/are correct?

(1)   The articles of association of a company limited by shares contain the internal regulations of the company

(2)   The articles of association form a contract between the shareholders and the company

A   1 only
B   2 only
C   Both 1 and 2
D   Neither 1 nor 2   (2 marks)

11.3   Which of the following clauses in the articles of association of Dee Ltd would NOT be enforceable against the company as a breach of contract?

A   Shareholders shall be paid dividends in cash
B   All shareholders are entitled to attend and vote at general meetings of the company
C   Tom (a shareholder) shall be the company's managing director for life   (1 mark)

11.4 **In the context of the articles of association which of the following statements is correct?**

(1)   They form a contract between the shareholders and the board of directors
(2)   They form a contract between the shareholders and the company
(3)   They form a contract between each shareholder and the other shareholders
(4)   They are only contractual in respect of ordinary membership rights

A   1, 2 and 3
B   1, 2 and 4
C   1, 3 and 4
D   2, 3 and 4   (2 marks)

11.5 **In relation to the Memorandum of Association, which of the following is correct?**

A   It must always be signed by a minimum of two subscribers
B   It may include an objects clause, but this is not mandatory
C   It confirms that the company is unlimited or limited
D   It is a now a historical document that can never be changed   (2 marks)

11.6 **Which of the following applies to entrenchment of articles of association?**

A   Any new entrenched provisions must be registered with the Registrar of Companies
B   It is no longer possible to create new entrenched articles of association
C   Entrenched articles of association can only be varied if a general meeting takes place   (1 mark)

11.7 **Which of the following statements relating to the memorandum of association of a private company limited by shares is correct?**

A   It may be altered by special resolution
B   It may be altered by a written resolution
C   It cannot be altered   (1 mark)

11.8 **Which of the followings statements relating to the articles of association is/are correct?**

(1)   The articles cannot constitute a contract between the company and a third party
(2)   Relevant terms of the articles may be implied into the contract

A   1 only
B   2 only
C   Both 1 and 2
D   Neither 1 nore 2   (2 marks)

11.9   The articles of Dee Ltd, a property development company, states that the company has the power to further its objects and that the directors have authority to borrow up to £200,000.

The board has resolved to purchase a plot of land for £300,000. The Midwest Bank plc has agreed to make a loan of £250,000 to Dee Ltd to acquire the land.

Which of the following statements is correct?

A   The loan is void as Dee Ltd has acted *ultra vires*

B   As the directors have exceeded their authority, the bank cannot enforce repayment of the loan against Dee Ltd

C   As the directors have resolved to obtain the loan, the transaction is lawful

D   The loan is *ultra vires* and the directors will be personally liable unless their actions are ratified by the shareholders   (2 marks)

11.10 A promoter is forming a company and delivering documents to the Registrar of Companies.

Which of the following would be included in the Memorandum of Association of the company?

A   The objects clause
B   A statement of initial capital
C   Subscribers' declaration   (1 mark)

(15 marks)

MCQs 12 SHARES

12.1 The authorised share capital of Wye Ltd is £250,000 divided into 250,000 ordinary £1 shares. The market value of each share is £2. Angela and Brian are the only shareholders. Each has taken 50,000 shares and each has, so far, paid £10,000.

What is the issued share capital and paid-up share capital?

	Issued	*Paid-up*
A	£250,000	£100,000
B	£200,000	£20,000
C	£100,000	£20,000
D	£50,000	£10,000

       (2 marks)

12.2 **A company CANNOT generally do which of the following?**

A   Invest in other companies unless authorised by the article of incorporation
B   Be funded by loans
C   Hold treasury shares   (1 mark)

12.3 Mr Wally buys a share in a company on 1 January.

To whom does Mr Wally become contractually bound?

A   The company only
B   The members as on 1 January
C   The company and the present members
D   The company and the members as on 1 January   (2 marks)

12.4 **Which of the following statements is correct in relation to company shares?**

(1)   All ordinary shares must be voting shares
(2)   Preference shares never entitle the holder to a vote
(3)   All preference shares carry cumulative rights

A   1 only
B   2 only
C   3 only
D   Neither 1, 2 nor 3   (2 marks)

12.5 **To which of the following does the term "subscribers" refer?**

A   The founding members of a company
B   The ordinary shareholders of a company
C   All shareholders of a company   (1 mark)

12.6 **Which of the following describes a person who invests in both the shares and debentures of a company?**

    A   A member

    B   A creditor

    C   A member and a creditor   (1 mark)

12.7 **Which of the following statements concerning shares in a company are correct?**

    (1)   Shares are personal property of a shareholder

    (2)   A shareholder may hold a fraction of a share

    (3)   Two or more people may hold the same share

    A   1 and 2 only

    B   1 and 3 only

    C   2 and 3 only

    D   1, 2 and 3   (2 marks)

12.8 **What does issued share capital represent?**

    A   The extent of the company's funding by its members

    B   The market value of the company's net assets

    C   The amount of cash injected by the members   (1 mark)

12.9 **What type of share may give the right to cumulative dividends?**

    A   Ordinary share

    B   Preference share

    C   Treasury share   (1 mark)

12.10 The statutory model articles provide that votes may be first counted on a show of hands.

    Who can demand a ballot?

    (1)   The Chairman of the board

    (2)   Any director

    (3)   Any two or more members

    A   1 and 2 only

    B   1 and 3 only

    C   2 and 3 only

    D   1, 2 and 3   (2 marks)

(15 marks)

MCQs 13 CAPITAL MAINTENANCE

13.1 **Which of the following statements is correct in relation to an issue of new shares?**

    (1)   All new shares issued by a private company must be offered to the existing members first

    (2)   All shares issued for cash must be offered to the existing members first

    A   1 only

    B   2 only

    C   Neither 1 nor 2

    D   Both 1 and 2   (2 marks)

13.2 **Which of the following statements about share capital is/are correct?**

(1) Subscriber's shares in a public company do not have to be paid in cash

(2) Neither a private company nor a public company may issue shares at a discount unless the balance remains payable by the shareholder

A 1 only
B 2 only
C Both 1 and 2
D Neither 1 nor 2 (2 marks)

13.3 **Which of the following is correct in relation to a company issuing shares?**

A Any limited company may issue shares by way of a public offer
B The directors are responsible for alloting shares
C The increase in authorised capital must be confirmed by the court (1 mark)

13.4 The directors of Pen Ltd are proposing a capital reduction. They have made a statutory declaration and called a general meeting of members.

What kind of resolution is required to approve the capital reduction?

A Ordinary resolution
B Ordinary resolution with special notice
C Extraordinary resolution
D Special resolution (2 marks)

13.5 The members of RRR Ltd have been asked to delegate the right to allot a new class of shares to the directors.

What is the maximum period of time for which such a resolution may be effective?

A One year
B Five years
C Ten years
D Indefinitely (2 marks)

13.6 Simone is a member of YYY Ltd. She has received a letter from the company stating that the company is unable to pay a dividend this year, but the company will be issuing members with additional shares.

This is an example of which of the following?

A A rights issue
B Pre-emption rights
C A bonus share issue
D An issue of shares for zero consideration (2 marks)

13.7 **Which of the following will give rise to a share premium?**

A Issuing shares at a discount
B Issuing share at nominal value for full consideration
C Issuing shares at nominal value for part consideration
D Issuing shares for more than nominal value (2 marks)

13.8   For which of the following purposes may the share premium account be used?

   A   To pay dividends on all classes of shares
   B   To pay dividends to preference shareholders only
   C   To issue bonus shares to existing members   (1 mark)

13.9   What is a "scrip issue"?

   A   An issue of bonus shares
   B   An issue of partly-paid shares
   C   An issue of shares for non-cash consideration   (1 mark)

13.10   Which of the following would be regarded as an issue of shares for an improper purpose?

   (1)   An issue of shares in return for a non-cash consideration
   (2)   An issue of shares to enable the directors to maintain control of the board
   (3)   An issue of shares to prevent a take-over bid

   A   1 and 2 only
   B   1 and 3 only
   C   2 and 3 only
   D   1, 2 and 3   (2 marks)

13.11   In order for a private company to be able to purchase its own shares out of capital, the directors must declare that the company would be solvent if it were wound up after the reduction.

   To what period after the reduction does this solvency statement relate?

   A   6 months
   B   12 months
   C   18 months   (1 mark)

13.12   A private limited company's accumulated profits and losses include a revaluation surplus on a non-current asset.

   When can the directors declare a dividend to be satisfied wholly or partly by the distribution of the surplus?

   A   Never as such a surplus is never realised and cannot be distributed

   B   Only in a voluntary winding-up if there are surplus assets to pay to the members

   C   At any time since a private company's profits available for distribution includes unrealised profits

   D   Only when the surplus is realised   (2 marks)

13.13   XXX Ltd wishes to reduce its capital, but the company's articles of association expressly forbid this.

   Which of the following statements applies to XXX Ltd?

   A   It will only require an ordinary resolution to sanction the reduction in capital
   B   It may pass a special resolution to change the articles of association and then proceed
   C   It will require unanimous consent of the members to change the articles of association
   D   It may proceed with the reduction, irrespective of the content of the articles of association   (2 marks)

13.14 A company passes a resolution to reduce share capital which involves the repayment to a shareholder of his paid-up share capital.

Who may object to the reduction?

(1)   Members who did not vote in favour of the resolution
(2)   Creditors of the company

A   1 only
B   2 only
C   Neither 1 nor 2
D   Both 1 and 2   (2 marks)

13.15 In order to reduce its share capital, the directors of a private company must sign a declaration of the company's solvency.

To whom and when must this statement be made?

A   To the members with the special resolution to reduce capital
B   To the court in advance of passing a resolution to reduce capital
C   To the court after the resolution to reduce capital is passed
D   To the Registrar of Companies within 15 days following the resolution to reduce capital   (2 marks)

13.16 **Who may incur a civil liability if a company pays an excessive dividend?**

A   The directors of the company only
B   The members of the company only
C   Both the directors and the members   (1 mark)

                                                                 (27 marks)

MCQs 14 LOAN CAPITAL

14.1 **Which of the following statements about company charges is correct?**

A   A floating charge has priority over a fixed charge
B   Preferential creditors take priority over fixed charge-holders
C   A fixed charge has priority over a floating charge   (1 mark)

14.2 Two fixed charges have been registered over the same property.

What is the position with regard to the competing claims of the charge-holders?

A   The first charge in time has priority

B   The two charges rank equally

C   The two charges rank equally unless the second charge-holder knew of the first charge   (1 mark)

14.3 **Which of the following statements about a floating charge is correct?**

A It is a charge over a class of company assets which the company is unable to deal with freely in the ordinary course of business

B It must be registered with the Registrar of Companies within 21 days of its creation otherwise the charge is void against the other creditors

C It must be registered at the company's registered office in the register of charges, but a failure to do so does not affect the validity of the charge (1 mark)

14.4 Under the *Companies Act 2006* a floating charge is void against the liquidator and any creditor of the company unless particulars of it are registered with the Registrar of Companies.

Within how many days of its creation must a charge be registered?

A 14 days
B 15 days
C 21 days (1 mark)

14.5 XXX plc as entered into both fixed and floating charge contracts.

Which of the following is correct?

A All charges must be registered with the Registrar of Companies
B Only the fixed charges are required to be registered with the Registrar of Companies
C The statutory duty to register the charges lies with the charge-holder
D If the charges are not duly registered they become unenforceable in an insolvent winding-up (2 marks)

14.6 Four providers of long-term finance have advanced funds to ZZZ plc, secured by debentures.

Which of the following has the highest priority claim against the company in the event of liquidation?

A ABC Bank, whose floating charge was created on 1 April and registered on 10 April
B DEF Finance, whose fixed charge was created on 5 April and registered on 9 April
C PQR Trust, whose fixed charge was created on 6 April and registered on 8 April
D XYZ Bank, whose floating charge was created on 30 March and registered on 7 April (2 marks)

14.7 TTT plc entered into a debenture secured by a floating charge on 3 June.

What is the latest date by which the charge must be registered?

A 11 June
B 14 June
C 24 June
D 1 July (2 marks)

14.8 UUU Finance Ltd is to lend money to a client company; the borrowing will be secured by way of a fixed charge. The lending officer of UUU Finance Ltd has the following documents:

(1) The client's memorandum of association
(2) The client's articles of association
(3) The draft debenture

Which of these documents form part of the binding agreement between UUU Finance Ltd and its client?

A 2 and 3 only
B 1 and 3 only
C 1 and 2 only
D 3 only   (2 marks)

14.9 On 10 September, solicitors representing BBB Bank plc and PQR Ltd confirmed that their clients would enter into a fixed charge. The parties signed the contract on 12 September. On 14 September, PQR Ltd noted the debenture in the company registers, and the debenture was finally registered at the Registrar of Companies on 19 September.

Which date is relevant to confirming the priority of the bank's charge against other creditors?

A 10 September
B 12 September
C 14 September
D 19 September   (2 marks)

14.10 Which of the following is LEAST suitable as security for a fixed charge?

A Plant and machinery
B Undeveloped land
C Stock-in-trade   (1 mark)

14.11 Frank, a shareholder of YYY Ltd, wishes to inspect the company's records to ascertain whether the company has any major borrowings secured against its assets.

Which of the following is correct?

A Frank has no entitlement to inspect the company records

B Frank may obtain details of total secured borrowings by way of charges, but not the specify details of individual charges

C Frank may obtain details of all charges over the assets of the company, but the company may ask for a fee for this service

D Frank may obtain details of all charges over the assets of the company, and he is legally entitled to do so free of charge   (2 marks)

14.12 When does a floating charge attach to the assets of a debtor company, if at all?

A Never
B When created
C On registration
D In the event of default   (2 marks)

14.13   RRR Bank plc holds a charge over the assets of VVV Ltd as security for its overdraft. The agreement between the parties specifies that interest is fixed at 10% for the duration of the two-year agreement and that amounts receivable from VVV Ltd's major customers will be applied to reduce the overdraft.

What type of charge is this?

A   A fixed charge as VVV Ltd must pay a fixed rate of interest
B   A fixed charge over the book debts of VVV Ltd
C   A floating charge over the book debts of VVV Ltd
D   A floating charge over all the current assets of VVV Ltd   (2 marks)

14.14   **Which of the following describes a debenture?**

A   Any form of secured debt
B   A written acknowledgement of a debt
C   All fixed and floating charges   (1 mark)

(22 marks)

MCQs 15 DIRECTORS

15.1   Zed plc holds its board meetings on the fifteenth day of each month. At the meeting on 15 June, the board discussed a potential contract with RST Ltd. On 1 July, Lucy, a director of Zed plc, bought shares in RST Ltd. On 25 July, Zed plc contracted with RST Ltd.

When should Lucy have declared her interest to the board of Zed plc?

A   15 June
B   1 July
C   15 July
D   15 August   (2 marks)

15.2   **Which of the following is required if the members of a company wish to remove a director?**

A   Ordinary resolution with ordinary notice
B   Ordinary resolution with special notice
C   Special resolution with ordinary notice   (1 mark)

15.3   **Which of the following statements about a company's borrowing powers are correct?**

(1)   A board resolution to borrow money is binding on the company
(2)   A decision by the managing director to borrow money is binding on the company
(3)   The shareholders may veto any decision to borrow money by passing an ordinary resolution

A   1 only
B   1 and 2 only
C   1 and 3 only
D   2 and 3 only   (2 marks)

15.4   **On what basis is a company liable for contracts entered into on its behalf by the board of directors?**

A   Vicarious liability
B   Companies legislation
C   The law of agency   (1 mark)

15.5   **Which of the following are correct?**

(1)   The first directors are appointed by a resolution of the members at the company's first Annual General Meeting

(2)   A director is regarded in law as a person who occupies the position of director by whatever title he is given

(3)   A shadow director is a person in accordance with whose directions or instructions the directors of the company are accustomed to act

A   1 and 2 only
B   1 and 3 only
C   2 and 3 only
D   All three statements   (2 marks)

15.6   **Which of the following statements regarding the directors' right to salary is correct?**

(1)   Directors may vote themselves such salary payments as they think fit, irrespective of anything in the company's articles of association

(2)   Directors are only entitled to be paid a salary for their services if the constitution of the company so provides

(3)   All directors must be paid a salary

A   1 only
B   2 only
C   1 and 2 only
D   3 only   (2 marks)

15.7   **Under the Companies Act 2006 which of the following must be notified to the Registrar of Companies in the prescribed form within fourteen days of occurrence?**

A   A change in the particulars of directors
B   A change in a director's interest in the company's shares
C   The approval of a director's service contract for more than five years   (1 mark)

15.8   **Under the Companies Act 2006 who can enforce the general duties owed by a director?**

(1)   The majority shareholders
(2)   The company
(3)   Individual directors

A   1 and 2 only
B   2 only
C   2 and 3 only
D   3 only   (2 marks)

15.9   Jack has acted in breach of his duty as a director of JK Ltd. The breach does not amount to fraud on the minority.

Which of the following is correct?

A   The breach cannot be ratified by the members
B   The breach may be ratified by a written or ordinary resolution
C   The breach may be ratified by a resolution of the board of directors   (1 mark)

15.10 **To which of the following are directors' duties owed?**

(1)   The company as a whole
(2)   Current individual shareholders
(3)   All the present and future individual shareholders

A   1 only
B   2 only
C   1 and 2 only
D   1, 2 and 3   (2 marks)

15.11 **In which of the following circumstances can a director's appointment be terminated?**

A   Personal bankruptcy
B   Personal illness
C   Death of spouse   (1 mark)

15.12 **What is the minimum age, if any, from which an individual may serve as a company director?**

A   There is no statutory minimum age
B   16 years
C   18 years   (1 mark)

15.13 **What is the minimum number of directors for private and public limited companies?**

	Private	*Public*
A	One	One
B	One	Two
C	Two	Two
D	Two	Three

(2 marks)

15.14 Stavros was the chief executive officer (CEO) of TTT Ltd, but resigned in order to establish his own company. Once the company was formed, he tendered successfully for a contract of which he became aware when attending a confidential meeting on behalf of TTT Ltd in his capacity as CEO. Stavros' new company made a substantial profit.

Which of the following is a consequence of Stavros' actions?

A   Any profit made by the new company can be claimed by TTT Ltd

B   Stavros was entitled to form the new company and accept the tender, so TTT Ltd has no recourse

C   Stavros can be prosecuted for his use of confidential information after leaving TTT Ltd

D   Stavros has no liability as his company has a separate legal personality   (2 marks)

15.15 **Under the Companies Act 2006, which of the following is a correct statement about the position of shadow directors?**

A   It is illegal to act as a shadow director
B   Particulars of shadow directors must be registered with the Registrar of Companies
C   A shadow director has the same obligations as a *de facto* director of the company

(1 mark)

(23 marks)

MCQs 16 OTHER COMPANY OFFICERS

16.1	**Which of the following statements about advice given by an auditor is correct?**

(1)	Auditors who provide negligent advice may be held liable for breach of contract by the company which appointed them

(2)	Auditors who provide negligent advice to the company which appointed them may be held liable for breach of contract by the company and its individual shareholders

(3)	Auditors who provide advice to an individual and know how the advice will be used may be held liable if they are negligent in giving that advice

A	1 only
B	1 and 2 only
C	1 and 3 only
D	2 and 3 only	(2 marks)

16.2	**Who is legally obliged to maintain a company's appropriate accounting records?**

A	The auditor
B	The company secretary
C	The finance director
D	The directors	(2 marks)

16.3	**Which of the following statements is correct in relation to company secretaries?**

A	A company secretary must be a natural person
B	The company secretary cannot also be a director of the same company
C	All companies must appoint a secretary
D	All company secretaries must be qualified by examination or experience	(2 marks)

16.4	**Which of the following is a routine duty of a company secretary?**

A	Maintaining order at general meetings
B	Setting the agenda for board meetings and general meetings
C	Liaison between the company and the Registrar of Companies	(1 mark)

16.5	**How can a company's external auditor be removed by the members?**

A	Ordinary resolution with ordinary notice
B	Ordinary resolution with special notice
C	Special resolution with ordinary notice	(1 mark)

16.6	Dev is the company Secretary of LLL plc. He entered into a contract to rent cars for use by the sales team. However, the directors of the company objected to what they considered to be an excessive price and refused to pay.

Can the car rental company enforce the payment?

A	The car rental company will not be able to enforce the payment as the board of directors of LLL plc have refused to sanction it

B	The car rental company can successfully claim that Dev had apparent authority to enter into the contract as he showed his business card before signing it

C	The car rental company cannot enforce the contract because a company Secretary has no authority to enter into contracts on behalf of the company

D	The car rental company can enforce the contract as Dev had implied actual authority arising from his position	(2 marks)

16.7 **Under the Companies Act 2006, which of the following is duty of an auditor?**

    A   To prevent and detect fraud in the client company

    B   To check all transactions of the client company

    C   To report on the financial statements of the client company   (1 mark)

16.8 **Under the provisions of the Companies Act 2006, to be eligible to be an auditor, an individual must be a member of which of the following?**

    A   A professional institute or association

    B   A self-regulatory body

    C   A recognised supervisory body   (1 mark)

16.9 Cabbit Ltd buys organic vegetables from farmers and resells them to retail outlets.

Which of the following accounting records must Cabbit Ltd maintain in order to comply with the Companies Act 2006?

    (1)   A record of its assets and liabilities

    (2)   A statement of stock held at the end of each financial year

    (3)   Daily entries of income and expenditure

    A   1 and 2 only

    B   1 and 3 only

    C   2 and 3 only

    D   1, 2 and 3   (2 marks)

16.10 A properly appointed company secretary signs two contracts:

    (1)   An employment contract with a factory worker

    (2)   A contract to purchase a property on behalf of the company

Which of these contracts are binding?

    A   1 only

    B   2 only

    C   Both 1 and 2

    D   Neither 1 nor 2   (2 marks)

16.11 Ben Ltd is a micro company and Dom Ltd is a small company.

Which of the following is a compulsory filing requirement for BOTH companies?

    (1)   Balance sheet

    (2)   Profit and loss account

    (3)   Directors' report

    (4)   Auditor's report

    A   1 only

    B   1 and 2 only

    C   1, 2 and 3

    D   1, 2 and 4   (2 marks)

(18 marks)

MCQs 17 COMPANY MEETINGS AND RESOLUTIONS

17.1 **Which of the following statements about a change of name of a company is NOT true?**

A	Change of name of a company requires special resolution
B	A resolution to change the name must be kept for at least 10 years
C	A name change can be passed by an ordinary resolution

(1 mark)

17.2 At a recent shareholders' meeting Pallas Ltd passed a special resolution to alter its class rights. Alf, Bert, Chris and Don own respectively 5%, 3%, 6% and 10% of the nominal value of the company's shares. Chris voted in favour of the resolution at the meeting but has subsequently changed his mind and, along with the others, wishes to object to the alteration.

Which of the following combinations of shareholders can apply to the court to have the alteration set aside?

A	Alf, Bert and Chris
B	Chris and Don
C	Bert, Chris and Don
D	Alf and Don

(2 marks)

17.3 **In relation to a written resolution, which of the following statements is correct?**

A	A written resolution must be passed by all the members
B	A written resolution applies only to private companies
C	Members need at least 25% of total voting rights to propose a written resolution
D	Any resolution may be a written resolution

(2 marks)

17.4 Bee Ltd has an issued share capital of 1,000 ordinary shares of £1 each. Some of the shareholders would like to pass a resolution to remove a director.

What is the minimum number of votes which must be cast in order to pass the resolution?

A	500
B	501
C	750
D	751

(2 marks)

17.5 **By what resolution may a director of a private company be removed by the shareholders?**

A	Ordinary resolution
B	Special resolution
C	Written resolution

(1 mark)

17.6 Some members of a public company wish to requisition a general meeting.

What proportion of the paid-up voting capital must they hold?

A	At least 5%
B	At least 10%
C	At least 25%
D	At least 50%

(2 marks)

17.7 In relation to the Annual General Meeting (AGM) of a public company which of the following statements is correct?

A   The first AGM must be held within 15 months of its incorporation

B   The gap between AGMs must not exceed 13 months

C   At least 21 days' notice must always be given to the members

D   The agenda is set by the directors   (2 marks)

17.8 For a public company, what is the minimum percentage of voting rights that must be held by a member for that member to request a resolution on the agenda for the next Annual General Meeting?

A   3%

B   5%

C   No minimum percentage required   (1 mark)

17.9 What is the required days of notice for a general shareholder meeting that is NOT an annual meeting?

A   14 days

B   21 days

C   None   (1 mark)

17.10 How many members are required to demand a poll at a general meeting under the Model Articles?

A   One

B   Two

C   Five   (1 mark)

17.11 Sarah, a member of XYZ plc, wishes to nominate Janis to attend the Annual General Meeting of XYZ plc as her proxy.

Which of the following statements is correct?

A   Janis must also be a member of XYZ plc

B   Sarah can only nominate a proxy if the articles of association allow this

C   Sarah will not be able to control how Janis votes

D   Only the chairman of the meeting may act as Sarah's proxy   (2 marks)

17.12 Which of the following matters would require a special resolution at a general meeting?

A   Change of name of the company

B   Removal of a director from the board

C   Increase in share capital of the company   (1 mark)

17.13 Special notice of a general meeting is required for which of the following resolutions?

A   Removal of the auditor

B   Repurchase of shares

C   Change of registered office   (1 mark)

17.14 Exactly 100 members attended the annual general meeting of JKL plc.

Assuming no postal votes were submitted, how many members would have been required to support a resolution to remove a director of the company?

A   50
B   51
C   75
D   76   (2 marks)

(21 marks)

MCQs 18 INSOLVENCY AND ADMINISTRATION

18.1 Immediately before XY Ltd was placed in insolvent liquidation, Alex, the company's sole director, arranged for the company to make an early repayment of an unsecured loan of £15,000 which he had provided to the company.

Which of the following is correct?

A   The repayment may have created a preference and Alex may have to return the £15,000 to XY Ltd

B   Alex may be fined

C   The repayment of the loan is valid so long as Alex was acting in good faith

D   XY Ltd and Alex may be guilty of fraud   (2 marks)

18.2 A company carries on business at a time when the directors ought to have known that insolvency was inevitable.

Who may be liable to contribute to the assets of the company?

(1)   The current directors
(2)   The shareholders of the company
(3)   The former directors of the company

A   1 only
B   1 and 2 only
C   1 and 3 only
D   1, 2 and 3   (2 marks)

18.3 A registered company with current assets of £5,000, trade creditors worth £10,000 and an unsecured bank overdraft of £10,000 sought an increase in its overdraft facility to £15,000. The bank agreed on the condition that it was given a floating charge over all the company's assets to secure the overdraft. The overdraft was repayable on demand if requested. The company was wound up three months later.

What sum is the bank entitled to as a secured creditor?

A   Nil
B   £5,000
C   £10,000
D   £15,000   (2 marks)

18.4   Neil has been allotted 500 £1 ordinary shares in Rogers Ltd. He has paid-up 70p per share.

What is Neil's liability in the event of Rogers Ltd being wound up?

A   £150
B   £350
C   £500   (1 mark)

18.5   **Who may nominate the liquidator in a creditors' voluntary liquidation?**

(1)   The creditors
(2)   The court
(3)   The members

A   1 only
B   1 and 2 only
C   1 and 3 only
D   1, 2 and 3   (2 marks)

18.6   **Who has immediate responsibility for dealing with the affairs of a company once a compulsory winding up order has been granted?**

A   The Official Receiver
B   The liquidator
C   An administrator   (1 mark)

18.7   RRR Ltd has defaulted on a floating charge. A court order has started administration proceedings.

Which of the following actions is the charge-holder entitled to take?

A   Appoint an administrator
B   Seize all of the assets of RRR Ltd
C   Obtain title to the assets of RRR Ltd, subject to a court order
D   Enter RRR Ltd's premises to secure the specific assets charged to him   (2 marks)

18.8   **Which of the following could be a ground for "just and equitable winding up"?**

A   All members agree that the company should pursue completely different objectives
B   One or more members are prevented from participating in operational decisions
C   The company has made no transactions for at least 12 consecutive months
                                                                                                 (1 mark)

18.9   EEE Ltd is in insolvent administration.

For which of the following will the administrator require permission from the court?

A   To permit a director of the company to remain in office
B   To make payments to preferred creditors
C   To take on the powers of the directors
D   To discharge accounts payable to unsecured creditors   (2 marks)

18.10   Marcel is the majority shareholder in Cook Restaurant Ltd. He wishes to retire and close down the business completely, as none of his family wish to succeed him. The company has creditors, but Marcel knows that the business is solvent and that the net assets will meet all obligations.

Which of the following is most appropriate to bring the company's existence to an end?

A   Creditors' voluntary liquidation
B   Administration
C   Creditors' compulsory liquidation
D   Members' voluntary liquidation   (2 marks)

18.11   **Which of the following is/are grounds for administration procedures?**

(1)   To put a rescue plan in place if it is possible to rescue the company, in whole or in part, as a going concern

(2)   If corporate rescue is not possible, to maximise the recovery of assets for the creditors

A   1 only
B   2 only
C   Neither 1 nor 2
D   Both 1 and 2   (2 marks)

18.12   **Which of the following is/are grounds for petitioning the court for compulsorily liquidation of a company?**

(1)   Members have passed a special resolution to seek compulsory liquidation
(2)   A public company fails to obtain a trading certificate within one year of incorporation

A   1 only
B   2 only
C   Neither 1 nor 2
D   Both 1 and 2   (2 marks)

18.13   In the event of liquidation the liquidator will distribute the company's assets in accordance with the priority determined by the law relating to insolvency.

Assuming there are surplus assets who ranks last in the priority of creditors?

A   Unsecured creditors
B   Ordinary shareholders
C   Floating charge-holders   (1 mark)

18.14   **What is the role of the Official Receiver?**

A   To appoint an insolvency practitioner to deal with a compulsory winding up order
B   To realise company assets for a floating charge-holder
C   To rescue a company as a going concern
D   To liquidate the assets of an insolvent company   (2 marks)

18.15 **Who ranks first in the order of priority of creditors when a company is in insolvency procedures?**

A The insolvency practitioner
B Fixed charge-holders
C Preferential debts
D The "prescribed part" (2 marks)

18.16 TTT Bank plc has a fixed charge over the assets of FFF Company. The total amount due to the bank is £50,000, but the value of the asset offered as security has fallen to £40,000.

What claim does TTT Bank plc have in the priority of creditors?

A First priority for £50,000
B First priority for £40,000 with no claim for the remainder
C First priority for £40,000 and a floating charge-holder claim for the remainder
D First priority for £40,000 with an unsecured creditor claim for the remainder
 (2 marks)

18.17 **In relation to company insolvency, what is the effect of an administration order?**

A The company will be liquidated following due process

B The company must pay its creditors, or make an arrangement with them, within 21 days

C The obligations of the company will be "ring-fenced" for a period specified by the court

D The Official Receiver is obliged to appoint a liquidator (2 marks)

18.18 **Which of the following may be arranged under "pre-pack" administration?**

(1) Potential buyers for the sale of the company
(2) A sale price for the business

A 1 only
B 2 only
C Neither 1 nor 2
D Both 1 and 2 (2 marks)

18.19 **When is a declaration of solvency required?**

A In a members' voluntary liquidation only
B In a creditors' voluntary liquidation and members' voluntary liquidation
C In a creditors' voluntary liquidation only (1 mark)

18.20 Jarvis & Co has been appointed as liquidator of JKL Ltd, a small manufacturing company, under a compulsory winding up order.

Who appointed Jarvis & Co?

A The court
B The Official Receiver
C The creditors of JKL Ltd
D The directors of JKL Ltd (2 marks)

18.21   **Which of the following is a false statement about the liquidator position?**

    A   The liquidator is not treated as an officer of the company for liability purposes

    B   The liquidator takes charge of and realises the company's assets

    C   The liquidator pays creditors of the company in statutory order   (1 mark)

(36 marks)

MCQs 19 FRAUDULENT AND CRIMINAL BEHAVIOUR

19.1   **When may directors be held liable to contribute to the assets of an insolvent company in respect of "wrongful trading"?**

    A   When the directors have the intention of defrauding creditors

    B   Whenever a company's liabilities exceed its assets

    C   Whenever a company becomes insolvent

    D   When the directors knew or ought to have known that insolvency was inevitable   (2 marks)

19.2   The court has decided that Jill, a director of Jay Ltd, has been wrongfully trading.

    What are the possible consequences for Jill?

    A   She may be fined

    B   She may be imprisoned

    C   She may be required to contribute to the assets of Jay Ltd

    D   She may be required to sell her shares in Jay Ltd   (2 marks)

19.3   On winding up a company it is discovered that it has been trading when the directors knew that insolvent liquidation could not be avoided.

    For which of the following actions may the directors be liable to contribute to the funds of the company?

    A   Wrongful trading

    B   Fraudulent trading

    C   Illegal dealing

    D   Market abuse   (2 marks)

19.4   **Which type of action, civil, criminal, or both, can be taken in relation to each of fraudulent trading and wrongful trading?**

	Fraudulent trading	*Wrongful trading*
A	Civil only	Criminal only
B	Criminal only	Civil only
C	Criminal only	Civil and criminal
D	Civil and criminal	Civil only

    (2 marks)

19.5   **Which of the following are broad categories of offence set out in the Bribery Act 2010?**

    (1)   Bribery of a foreign public official

    (2)   Bribery of a UK public official

    (3)   Failure by a company to prevent a bribe being paid on its behalf

    (4)   Offering, promising or giving an advantage

A	1 and 4 only
B	2 and 4 only
C	1, 3 and 4
D	2, 3 and 4

(2 marks)

19.6 A UK-based company was bidding for a major haulage contract. Without the knowledge of the owners or management one of its employees paid a bribe to ensure the award of the contract.

Who may be prosecuted and on what grounds?

(1) The company, for failing to prevent bribery
(2) The employee, for giving a bribe

A	1 only
B	2 only
C	Neither 1 nor 2
D	Both 1 and 2

(2 marks)

19.7 Under the Bribery Act 2010, a commercial organisation will be liable if a person who is "associated" with it commits an offence under the Act.

Who is likely to be an "associated" person?

(1) An independent contractor who performs services for the organisation
(2) An agent who deals with the organisations' customers
(3) A supplier from which the organisation buys goods only

A	1 and 2 only
B	1 and 3 only
C	2 and 3 only
D	1, 2 and 3

(2 marks)

19.8 **Under the Bribery Act 2010, what policy should businesses follow?**

A	Bribery is never acceptable
B	Bribery is only acceptable in overseas areas where it is part of the culture
C	Whether or not bribery is acceptable needs to be determined on a case by case basis
D	Bribery is acceptable in certain limited circumstances

(2 marks)

19.9 An effective communication of an organisations' commitment to zero tolerance of bribery is an example of an anti-bribery measure.

Which of the following would NOT be included in this communication?

A	The consequences of breaching the bribery policy or contractual provisions relating to bribery prevention for employees and associated persons respectively
B	The names of previous employees that have been involved in bribery and the punishments they received
C	Reference to the bribery prevention procedures in place or being put in place
D	A commitment to carry out business honestly

(2 marks)

19.10   A fund manager who has acquired some price sensitive information on a company takeover from a stock market trader buys and sells shares on the basis of that information.

Is he guilty of insider dealing?

A   No, because the trader's information will be widely available in the market
B   Yes, because the information is not widely available in the market
C   No, but the trader could be
D   Yes, unless he makes a loss on the transactions   (2 marks)

19.11   **Which of the following is specifically a criminal offence under the Companies Act 2006?**

A   Bribery
B   Fraudulent trading
C   Money laundering
D   Wrongful trading   (2 marks)

19.12   Nathan works as an accountant in Moneyneeds Ltd, a financial services company. He is asked to prepare some accounts which he strongly suspects are going to be used to enable the company to evade some of its tax liability. He makes a report to the Money Laundering Reporting Officer nominated by his employer but, in fear of losing his job, he also prepares the accounts as required.

What offence has he committed under the Proceeds of Crime Act 2002?

A   Money laundering only
B   Tipping off only
C   Money laundering and tipping off
D   He has not committed any offence   (2 marks)

19.13   Marco runs a language training college. He deposits the proceeds of his criminal activities alongside the legitimate receipts of the college, and then disperses the funds through several overseas bank accounts.

What offence is Marco committing?

A   Wrongful trading
B   Fraud
C   Money laundering
D   Fraudulent trading   (2 marks)

19.14   Frank acts as an agent for Marilyn, purchasing nightwear from a number of different suppliers. Sometimes the suppliers pay a commission on orders placed with them by Frank on behalf of Marilyn. Frank regards the commissions as a perk of the job and keeps them.

Which of the following describes the legal position?

A   Marilyn may dismiss Frank and recover the amount of commissions retained by him

B   Commissions are customarily retained by an agent and so Frank has no liability in respect of them

C   Marilyn can take action against the suppliers for directing the commissions to Frank instead of her

D   The commissions are bribes and Marilyn should report Frank to the police

                                                                          (2 marks)

19.15 The Companies Act 2006 includes provisions relating to fraudulent trading.

Which of the following statements is/are correct?

(1) The Companies Act 2006 provisions only apply if a business was carried on with intent to defraud or for any fraudulent purpose

(2) A company officer who obtains further borrowing for the company, when he suspects that the company may not be able to repay it, may be convicted of fraudulent trading

A 1 only
B 2 only
C Neither 1 or 2
D Both 1 and 2 (2 marks)

19.16 **In relation to the criminal offence of bribery, which of the following statements is/are correct?**

(1) Offering favours to a person in public office in order to circumvent the ethical guidelines of his professional body is an offence

(2) Bribery may be punished by a term of imprisonment or a fine

A 1 only
B 2 only
C Neither 1 or 2
D Both 1 and 2 (2 marks)

19.17 **In the context of alleged bribery offences, which TWO of the following statements in relation to a deferred prosecution agreement are correct?**

(1) It automatically suspends prosecution proceedings
(2) It is available to individual persons and legal entities
(3) It does not avoid the financial consequences of the offence
(4) It can be proposed even if there is insufficient evidence to prosecute

A 1 and 3
B 1 and 4
C 2 and 3
D 2 and 4 (2 marks)

(34 marks)

Question 1 BIZZY LTD

Bizzy Ltd operates a building construction business. During the course of a new building development some scaffolding collapses and a number of employees are injured. Their injuries would have been greater if a warning shouted by the works foreman had not enabled them to start moving away from the building.

However, two employees, Dennis and Sam, received more serious injuries. Dennis is deaf and did not hear the warning and Sam, contrary to instructions, was not wearing a safety helmet.

Required:

(a)	State what is meant by "standard of care".	(2 marks)
(b)	State the standard of care that Bizzy Ltd owed to Dennis and to Sam.	(2 marks)
(c)	Explain a defence that may reduce the liability of Bizzy Ltd for a claim of negligence by Sam.	(2 marks)

(6 marks)

Question 2 PROFESSOR PARFITT

Parfitt, a professor in accountancy, lectures the principles of financial investment to university students. By way of example, he mentioned that Expand plc looked like a company that offered great investment potential. Frank, one of Parfitt's students, told his friend Rusty and they both invested their savings in Expand plc. Some months later the company was reported to be in serious financial difficulties and they do not expect to recover any of their investment.

Required:

(a)	State the tests that must be satisfied for a duty of care to exist.	(2 marks)
(b)	Explain whether Parfitt is liable to Frank and Rusty.	(4 marks)

(6 marks)

Question 3 GREGORY, DOUGLAS AND MICHAEL

Gregory owned a piece of land on which he decided to build a petrol station and garage. He constructed a large underground storage tank designed by Douglas, a civil engineer. Owing to a defect in the design of the tank a significant amount of petrol leaked into the surrounding land.

This was only discovered when a neighbour, Michael, was lighting a barbeque in his garden. The resulting fire completely destroyed Michael's house. Michael is seeking to claim damages from Gregory for the cost of rebuilding his home.

Required:

(a)	State the liability of Douglas to Gregory.	(2 marks)
(b)	State the liability of Douglas to Michael.	(2 marks)
(c)	State Gregory's liability for damages claimed by Michael.	(2 marks)

(6 marks)

Question 4 ESCAPADE LTD

Escapade Ltd has recently opened a paintball games centre in Kingsdale. Andrew took a group of friends there on his birthday. They were given a safety demonstration on how to use the "guns" to shoot small plastic paint balls that explode on impact. They were warned not to shoot at close range as the paintballs could cause serious bruising.

During the course of a game Andrew was hit at close range on his knee. This caused him to leap backwards into a fence. The fence had not been erected securely and he fell through it, breaking his arm.

Required:

(a)   State the defence *volenti non fit injuria*.   (2 marks)

(b)   Explain whether Escapade Ltd will be liable to Andrew for his injuries.   (4 marks)

                                                                              (6 marks)

Question 5 NETSCAPE LTD AND NETSCOPE LTD

Mat is considering setting up a new internet cafe as a private limited company. He also thinks that as there is an existing business called Netscape Ltd it would be a good idea to call his new company Netscope Ltd in the chance that he could transfer some of its business to his new company.

Required:

(a)   State the two ways in which "passing off" can arise.   (2 marks)

(b)   State how tort law protects Netscape Ltd's business.   (2 marks)

(c)   State whether Mat will be liable under tort law if he uses the name Netscope Ltd.

                                                                              (2 marks)

                                                                              (6 marks)

Question 6 HELEN & INGRID

Helen is a fine art dealer. She receives a circular letter from a fellow-dealer, Ingrid, stating that Ingrid has a painting by Gerald for sale.   Ingrid indicates a price of £1,000.

Helen telephones Ingrid and tells her that she is prepared to buy the painting for £750. Ingrid replies that she is not prepared to sell the painting for less than £900. Helen says she will think about it.

Later that day, James, a regular customer of Helen's, asks her if she has anything available by Gerald. She offers him the painting for £2,000 and he agrees to buy it, sight unseen.

Helen telephones Ingrid, to confirm that she will take the picture for the original £1,000 asking price. Ingrid replies that she has now sold the picture to another dealer, Kate, for £1,200.

Required:

In the context of contract law:

(a)   Explain Helen's liability to James, if any.   (2 marks)

(b)   Explain whether any binding agreement exists between Helen and Ingrid.   (4 marks)

                                                                              (6 marks)

Question 7 ALAN

Alan is a qualified accountant. Last year he agreed with his father Ben, who owns a small manufacturing business, that he would prepare his tax return for him for a fee of £500. Alan did the accountancy work and Ben submitted the accounts to the tax authorities. Ben now refuses to pay Alan, saying that it is not right for a son to charge his father for doing him a favour.

Alan, in an attempt to encourage his daughter, Dawn, in her studies, promised that he would buy her a new car if she passed her final examinations. Although Dawn has now passed her exams, Alan is refusing to buy her the promised car.

Required:

(a)   **Explain whether Alan can require Ben to pay him for his accountancy work.**   (4 marks)

(b)   **Explain whether Dawn can require her father to buy her the new car.**   (2 marks)

(6 marks)

Question 8 AL & BASH CARS PLC

Al operates a small business manufacturing specialist engine filters. In January he placed an advertisement in a car trade magazine stating that he would supply filters at £60 per filter, but would consider a reduction in the price for substantial orders.

He received a letter from Bash Cars plc requesting his terms of supply for 1,000 filters. Al replied, offering to supply the filters at a cost of £50 each. Bash Cars plc responded to Al's letter stating that they accepted his offer but that they would only pay £45 per filter.

Al wrote back to Bash Cars plc stating that he would supply the filters but only at the original price of £50. When Al's letter arrived, the purchasing director of Bash Cars plc did not notice the alteration of the price and ordered the 1,000 filters from Al, which he supplied.

Required:

(a)   **Identity from the scenario above the invitations to treat, offers and counter-offers, if any.**   (4 marks)

(b)   **State what price, if any, Al is entitled to claim from Bash Cars plc.**   (2 marks)

(6 marks)

Question 9 AMI

In January 2016 Ami took over an old warehouse with the intention of opening an art gallery. As the warehouse had to be converted, Ami entered into a contract with Cis to do all the necessary painting. Cis was to be paid £5,000. Cis received an initial payment of £1,000 and agreed to have the work completed on 31 March.

At the end of February, Ami offered to pay Cis the sum of £1,000 to ensure that the job was done on time.

On completion of the work on time Ami refused to make the additional payment to Cis, beyond the original contractual price.

Required:

(a) State whether an enforceable contract exists between Cis and Ami under common law.

(2 marks)

(b) Explain whether Cis has a right in law to enforce Ami's promise to pay an extra £1,000.

(4 marks)

(6 marks)

Question 10 AMY & BEN

In January 2016, Amy started a business as an independent website designer.

To give her a start in her career, her brother Ben, who ran a retail business, said he would give her £1,000 if she updated his business website. However, by the time Amy had completed the two projects her design business had become a huge success and she had lots of other clients. When Ben discovered how successful Amy's business had become he felt that he should not be asked to pay for the work done for him. Ben said he would not pay anything as he had only offered the work to help his sister out.

Required:

(a) State the presumptions that are applied in relation to parties' intentions to create legal relations.

(2 marks)

(b) Explain whether Amy can insist that Ben pays the full amount of his initial promise.

(4 marks)

(6 marks)

Question 11 ADE

Ade, a pottery collector, saw a notice for an auction of Bede pottery. When he arrived to the auction house he found a notice outside, stating that the auction had been cancelled.

Ade went into a nearby antique shop and saw an item he liked. It bore a price ticket of £500. Ade said to the shopkeeper, Chip, that he was only willing to pay £350 for it. Chip, said he would sell it for £400 and as Ade said he would think about it over lunch. Chip agreed not to sell it before Ade returned.

However, when Ade returned, Chip had already sold the item to someone else for £450.

Required:

In the context of contract law:

(a) State whether Ade had received an offer from the auctioneers.

(2 marks)

(b) Explain whether Chip and Ade entered into an option contract.

(4 marks)

(6 marks)

Question 12 ALI

Ali is a dealer in Persian rugs. As his business has been rather slow, he placed an advertisement in the Saturday edition of his local paper stating:

"Once in a lifetime opportunity to own a handmade Persian antique rug for only £1,500 – cash only. This is a serious offer – the rug will go to the first person who accepts it – offer valid for one day only – today Saturday."

When Bud saw the advert, he immediately posted a letter of acceptance of Ali's offer in order to make sure he got the rug.

Later, Ed offered to pay £2,000 in cash for the rug and Ali sold the rug to him.

On Monday morning Bud's letter arrived.

Required:

In the context of the rules governing the creation of contracts:

(a)	**State the precise legal nature of Ali's advertisement;**	(2 marks)
(b)	**Explain whether Bud has entered into a legally-binding contract with Ali.**	(4 marks)

(6 marks)

Question 13 ANO LTD

Ano Ltd is a publisher specialising in producing scientific textbooks.

In January 2016, it decided to produce a new edition of a particular book and commissioned Box to provide the text. The contract entered into between Ano Ltd and Box required the text to be produced by 30 April 2016 and the fee agreed was £5,000.

In March 2016, Box informed Ano Ltd that he would not supply the finished text on time unless Ano Ltd increased his payment by £1,000. Ano Ltd agreed to the increase but when Box submitted his invoice on delivering the text, Ano Ltd refused to pay the additional amount.

Required:

In the context of the law of contract:

(a)	**State the rules of consideration.**	(2 marks)
(b)	**Explain whether Box can enforce the additional payment.**	(4 marks)

(6 marks)

Question 14 ABID

Abid regularly takes his car to be serviced at Bust Ltd. Before handing his car over to the garage, he is usually required to read and sign a contractual document which states:

"Bust Ltd accepts no responsibility for any consequential loss or injury sustained as a result of any work carried out by the company, whether as a result of negligence or otherwise."

On the most recent occasion, he was not asked to sign this document.

On driving home after its service, Abid was severely injured when the car's brakes failed. Bust Ltd has accepted that a mechanic was negligent but denies any liability for Abid's injuries, relying on the exclusion clause above.

Required:

(a) State TWO ways in which an exclusion clause can be incorporated into a contract.

                                       (2 marks)

(b) State whether Bust Ltd can claim reliance on an exclusion clause.   (2 marks)

(c) State the implications of the Consumer Rights Act 2015 for any claim Abid might make against Bust Ltd in relation to his injuries.   (2 marks)

                                         (6 marks)

Question 15 ANDRE

Andre entered into a contract with Bath Ltd to construct an outdoor swimming pool in his garden. The pool was to be 25 metres long by 10 metres wide by 2 metres deep, and was to be cleaned by a special non-chlorine based filter system.

When the pool was finished and Andre tried it for the first time. He found that it was only 1·80 metres deep and kept clean with chlorine. As a result, Andre, who unknown to Bath Ltd was highly allergic to chlorine, suffered a severe reaction and had to take a week off his work and as a result lost a potentially lucrative contract.

Required:

In the context of contract law:

(a) Explain whether Andre can require Bath Ltd to rectify the construction of the swimming pool. State what alternative action is available to him.   (4 marks)

(b) State what action Andre can take against Bath Ltd for the loss of the potentially lucrative contract.   (2 marks)

                                         (6 marks)

Question 16 ARI, BI & CAS

Ari operates a business as a designer of internet web pages for a variety of business clients. Unfortunately he has had some difficulty in recovering his full fees from two clients as follows:

(a) Bi, a newly qualified accountant, told Ari that although she could only raise the cash to pay half of the outstanding fees she would, as an alternative to paying the other half, do all of Ari's accountancy work for the coming year. Ari reluctantly agreed to this proposal.

(b) Cas, a self-employed musician, told Ari that she could not pay any of the money she owed him. However, her father offered to pay Ari, but could only manage half of the total amount owed. Once again Ari reluctantly agreed to accept the father's payment of the reduced sum.

Required:

In the context of contract law, explain whether Ari can recover any of the outstanding money from:

(a) Bi;   (3 marks)
(b) Cas.   (3 marks)

                                         (6 marks)

Question 17 AZ LTD

Az Ltd operates a shipbuilding business, which specialises in constructing and modifying ships to order. In 2016, the company entered into a contract to build a new ship for Cam for a total cost of £25 million. The contract terms provided that the total price was to be paid in 12 instalments and, in the event of Cam failing to make a payment, gave Az Ltd the right to terminate the agreement and claim an amount equal to 20% of the total contract price as damages. Any amount paid over the 20% was required to be returned to Cam.

Cam failed to make the first instalment payment, but refused to pay the damages as set out in the agreement on the grounds that they were excessive.

Required:

(a) **Identify the type of damages in the contract terms and state when these will be respected by the courts.** (2 marks)

(b) **Explain whether Az Ltd is likely to succeed in claiming damages from Cam.** (4 marks)

(6 marks)

Question 18 APT LTD

Apt Ltd is a small book company. In January 2015 it signed a contract with Bel, to publish her second book of poems in August 2016. In March 2015, Bel won a prestigious award for her first book of poems.

In the light of Bel's recent fame, Apt Ltd launched an extensive advertising campaign publicising the second book. The campaign was expensive, but successful . Apt Ltd won a contract to supply a large book club with 100,000 copies.

Unfortunately in May 2016, Bel informed Apt Ltd that she would not be able to supply the manuscript to it as she had signed a more rewarding contract with Cax plc, a very large publishing company.

Required:

(a) **Explain the nature of Bel's anticipatory breach of contract.** (4 marks)

(b) **State when and how Apt Ltd can respond to Bel's anticipatory breach of contract.** (2 marks)

(6 marks)

Question 19 DAI & CHRIS

Dai, a builder, employs Chris as a foreman to oversee his team of builders. Chris has some years' experience in the trade, and Dai is confident in entrusting him with the responsibility. However, after a few weeks it becomes apparent that Chris is failing to do the job as well as Dai had hoped or expected, and in consequence the team's work is falling behind schedule. He tries to discuss matters with Chris but the meeting ends in an argument and, in the heat of the moment, Dai dismisses him from his job.

Shortly after, Chris contacts Dai to tell him that he is bringing legal proceedings against Dai in relation to his dismissal.

Required:

(a)   **Explain the basis on which Chris would have a claim against Dai for unfair dismissal.**
                                                                                    (4 marks)

(b)   **If Chris was successful in a claim against Dai, state whether he can require that Chris reinstate him.**   (2 marks)

(6 marks)

Question 20 FITZ

Fitz ran a publishing business, which specialised in producing legal textbooks. Gus and Hilda both worked for Fitz as proof readers and editors for a period of three years. They were both described as self-employed and both paid tax as self-employed persons. Fitz provided all of their computer equipment.

Gus was required to work solely on the projects Fitz provided and attend Fitz's premises every day. Hilda usually worked at home and was allowed to work on other projects. Hilda could even arrange for her work for Fitz to be done by someone else if she was too busy to do it personally. Also Gus received payment when he could not work because of illness, but Hilda received no such payment.

Last month, Fitz decided to move out of the law textbook market and, instead, to specialise in scientific textbooks. As a result he told Gus and Hilda that there would be no more work for them.

Required:

(a)   **Explain why it is important to distinguish between contracts of service and contracts for services.**   (2 marks)

(b)   **State the "economic reality test".**   (2 marks)

(c)   **Explain how the economic reality test applies to Gus.**   (2 marks)

(6 marks)

Question 21 DAN

Dan operated a business providing statistical analysis in the financial services sector. Eve and Fred have both worked for Dan since they graduated from university three years ago. They were both described as self-employed and both paid tax as self-employed persons. Dan provided all of their specialist computer equipment and software. Eve was required to work solely on the projects Dan provided, and she had to attend Dan's premises every day from 9 am until 5 pm.

Fred, on the other hand, usually worked at home and was allowed to work on other projects. Fred could even arrange for his work for Dan to be done by someone else if he was too busy to do it personally.

As a result of the downturn in the financial services sector Dan has told Eve and Fred that there will be no more work for them and that they will not receive any further payment or compensation from him for their loss of work.

Required:

(a)   **State TWO tests developed by the courts to distinguish the employee from the self-employed.**   (2 marks)

(b)   **Explain Eve's and Fred's entitlement to redundancy payments.**   (4 marks)

(6 marks)

Question 22 GOAL LTD

Hope incorporated his property development company 12 months ago as Goal Ltd. On formation, Hope asked three of his business contacts to supply additional capital in return for which they became directors. Although never formally appointed, Hope took the role and title of chief executive and the other directors left the day-to-day running of the business to him and simply received feedback from him at board meetings.

Six months ago Hope entered into a contract, on Goal Ltd's behalf, with Ima to produce plans for the redevelopment of a particular site that it hoped to acquire. However, Goal Ltd did not acquire the site and due to its currently risky financial position and its fear of potential losses, the board of directors has refused to pay Ima, claiming that Hope did not have the necessary authority to enter into the contract with her.

Required:

(a)   **State how the power of the board of directors may be extended to individual directors.**

(3 marks)

(b)   **Explain whether the board of directors of Goal Ltd is liable on the contract with Ima.**

(3 marks)

(6 marks)

Question 23 CHI, DI & FI

Chi, Di and Fi formed an ordinary partnership to run an art gallery. Each of them paid £100,000 into the business. The partnership agreement specifically restricted the scope of the partnership business to the sale of "paintings, sculptures and other works of art".

In January 2016 Chi took £10,000 from the partnership's bank drawn on its overdraft facility. She had told the bank that the money was to finance a short-term partnership debt but in fact she used the money to pay for a holiday.

In February Di entered into a £25,000 contract on behalf of the partnership to buy some books, which she hoped to sell in the gallery.

Required:

(a)   **State the liability of partners for partnership debts in an ordinary partnership.** (2 marks)

(b)   **Explain the liabilities of Chi and Di arising from their actions.**   (4 marks)

(6 marks)

Question 24 GEO, HO & IO

Geo, Ho and Io formed a partnership three years ago to run a hairdressing business. They each provided capital to establish the business as follows:

Geo	£20,000
Ho	£12,000
Io	£8,000

The partnership agreement stated that all profits and losses were to be divided in proportion to the capital contribution.

After 18 months Geo provided the partnership with a loan of £3,000 in order to finance the purchase of more stock. The loan was to be paid back from the profits of the business.

Unfortunately the business was not successful and the partners decided to dissolve the partnership rather than risk running up any more losses. At the time of the dissolution of the partnership its assets were worth £20,000. Its external debts were £7,000 and none of the debt to Geo has ever been paid.

Required:

(a) State the partners' liabilities for the partnership's debts on dissolution. (2 marks)

(b) Explain how the creditors' claims will be met. (4 marks)

(6 marks)

Question 25 HAN, ITA & JO

In January 2016, Han, Ita and Jo formed a partnership, under the Partnership Act 1890, to run a pottery business trading under the name HIJ Potteries.

On formation, Han, Ita and Jo introduced £6,000, £3,000 and £1,000, respectively. They all actively participated in the operation of the business and the partnership agreement stated that all profits and losses should be divided in proportion to the capital contribution. However, as Jo was the person who would actually be making the pottery, it was agreed that she would not be liable for any more than her initial contribution towards any future debts.

After some time, Han provided the partnership with a loan of £1,000 in order to sustain the operation of the business.

Unfortunately, the business was not successful and made significant losses. The partners concluded that it would be best to stop trading and dissolve the partnership. Its assets were worth £5,000 and its external debts were £9,000.

Required:

(a) State the liabilities of the partners for the debts of HIJ Potteries. (2 marks)

(b) State the order in which proceeds from the dissolution of HIJ Potteries will be applied. (2 marks)

(c) State how the partners will be required to contribute to HIJ Potteries' debts. Calculations are NOT required. (2 marks)

(6 marks)

Question 26 FRANK

Frank is a businessman. Frank entered into an agreement to sell some goods to George. The contract document stated that the contract was made with George's company George Ltd. The goods have been delivered but not been paid for. George claims that his company, and not he, is responsible for any debts owed to Frank. George Ltd has just gone into insolvent liquidation.

Required:

(a) State what is meant by the doctrine of separate personality. (2 marks)

(b) State the consequences of separate personality. (2 marks)

(c) State the claims, if any, that Frank can make for repayment from George or George Ltd. (2 marks)

(6 marks)

Question 27 DOC

Doc, a supplier of building materials, entered into the following transactions:

(a)   An agreement to sell some goods to a long-standing friend, Ed. The contractual document, however, actually stated that the contract was made with Ed's company, Ed Ltd. Although the materials were delivered, they have not been paid for and Doc has learned that Ed Ltd has just gone into insolvent liquidation.

(b)   Doc had employed a salesman, Fitt, whose contract of employment contained a clause preventing Fitt from approaching any of Doc's clients for a period of two years after he had left Doc's employment. Doc has found out that, on ceasing to work for him, Fitt has started working for a company, Gen Ltd. Gen Ltd is wholly-owned by Fitt and his wife and is approaching client contacts Fitt had made while working for Doc.

Required:

Explain the implications of the doctrine of separate personality for each of the following:

(a)   **Doc's contract to sell goods to Ed;**   (3 marks)

(b)   **Gen Ltd's approaches to clients of Doc.**   (3 marks)

(6 marks)

Question 28 DON

Don was instrumental in forming Eden plc, which was registered and received its trading certificate six months ago. It has subsequently come to the attention of the board of directors that the following events had taken place prior to the incorporation of the company:

(i)   Don had sold the premises in which Eden plc was to conduct its business to the company without declaring his interest in the contract;

(ii)   Don entered into a contract in the company's name to buy computer equipment, which the board of directors do not wish to honour.

Required:

(a)   **State whether a pre-incorporation contract is legal binding on a company.**   (2 marks)

(b)   **State whether or not Don will be viewed as a promoter in relation to these two transactions.**   (2 marks)

(c)   **State what action, if any, Eden plc can take in relation to each of these transactions.**
                                                                               (2 marks)

(6 marks)

Question 29 FRED

Fred is a member of Glad Ltd, a small publishing company. He holds 100 of its 500 shares; the other 400 shares are held by four other members.

It has recently become apparent that Fred has set up a rival business to Glad Ltd and the other members have decided that he should be expelled from the company.

To that end they propose to alter the articles of association to include a new power to "require any member to transfer their shares for fair value to the other members on the passing of a resolution so to do".

Required:

(a) State the requirements for changing the articles of association of a company.   (2 marks)

(b) Explain whether the proposed changes to the articles of Glad Ltd will be legally enforceable.   (4 marks)

(6 marks)

Question 30 GILT LTD

Gilt Ltd has issued share capital of 100,000 £1 shares held by 100 members.

Harry, the managing director, has been approached by Itt plc in respect of a proposed takeover bid for Gilt Ltd. Itt plc has given Harry a "facility fee" of £50,000 for ensuring that the takeover is successful.

At the next board meeting Harry convinces the other directors that the takeover bid is in the long-term interest of Gilt Ltd. However, the board is concerned that the holders of the majority of the issued share capital will not approve of the takeover.

In order to ensure the success of the takeover, the directors of Gilt Ltd agree that they should allot sufficient new shares to Itt plc to ensure that a new majority of members will support the takeover.

After the allocation of the shares to Itt plc a general meeting is called to consider the takeover and it is approved, with Itt plc voting in favour.

Required:

(a) State the legality of Harry's acceptance of the facility fee.   (2 marks)

(b) Explain the legality of the allotment of new shares.   (4 marks)

(6 marks)

Question 31 DEE & EFF

Dee and Eff are major shareholders in, and the directors of, the public company, Fan plc. For the year ended 30 April 2015 Fan plc's financial statements showed a loss of £2,000 for the year.

For the year ended 30 April 2016 Fan plc made a profit of £3,000 and, due to a revaluation, the value of its land and buildings increased by £5,000.

As a consequence, Dee and Eff recommended, and the shareholders approved, the payment of £4,000 in dividends.

Required:

(a) Explain the restrictions imposed on distributions by Fan plc and the legality of the proposed dividend.   (4 marks)

(b) State the potential legal liabilities of the shareholders if the dividend is paid.   (2 marks)

(6 marks)

Question 32 HOT LTD

At the start of 2013, Hot Ltd entered into the following transactions in an endeavour to sustain its operation:

(1)   It borrowed £50,000 from Ina, secured by a floating charge. The floating charge was created on 1 April and properly registered on 15 April;

(2)   It borrowed a further £50,000 from Jo. This loan was secured by a floating charge created on 3 April that was properly registered on 12 April;

(3)   It borrowed £100,000 from Ko-Bank. This loan was secured by a fixed charge. It was created on 5 April and properly registered on 16 April.

Unfortunately, the money borrowed was not sufficient to sustain Hot Ltd and, in August 2016, compulsory liquidation proceedings began. It is extremely unlikely that there will be sufficient assets to pay the debts owed to all of the secured creditors.

Required:

(a)   **State how the following secure a loan to a company:**

   (i)   **Fixed charge; and**
   (ii)   **Floating charge.**   (2 marks)

(b)   **Explain the order of priority in which the three debts must be paid.**   (4 marks)

                                                                                          (6 marks)

Question 33 CLEAN LTD

Clean Ltd was established five years ago to manufacture industrial solvents and cleaning solutions and Des was appointed managing director.

The company's main contract was with Dank plc, a large industrial conglomerate.

In the course of its research activity, Clean Ltd's scientists developed a new super glue. Des was very keen to pursue the manufacture of the glue but the board of directors overruled him.

The managing director of Dank plc, Bret is a friend of Des's. Bret has told Des that Dank plc will not be renewing its contract with Clean Ltd but would be happy to continue to deal with Des, if only he was not linked to Clean Ltd.

Following that discussion Des resigned from Clean Ltd and set up his own company, Flush Ltd which later entered into a contract with Dank plc to replace Clean Ltd. Flush Ltd also manufactures the new glue discovered by Clean Ltd's scientists, which has proved to be very profitable.

Required:

In relation to company law:

(a)   **Identify when a conflict of interest may arise.**   (2 marks)

(b)   **State whether a conflict may be subsequently approved.**   (2 marks)

(c)   **Explain whether or not Des is liable to Clean Ltd.**   (2 marks)

                                                                                          (6 marks)

Question 34 CAZ

Caz is a director of Dull plc, but she also carries out her own business as a wholesale supplier of specialist metals under the name of Era Ltd.

Last year Dull plc entered into a contract to buy a large consignment of metal from Era Ltd. Caz attended the board meeting that approved the contract and voted in favour of it, without revealing any link with Era Ltd.

Required:

(a)   **Explain whether Caz had a duty to disclose her relationship with Era Ltd to the other board members.**   (4 marks)

(b)   **State Caz's liability, if any, that arises from her actions.**   (2 marks)

(6 marks)

Question 35 JUST LTD

In 2012 Ger was disqualified from acting as a company director for a period of 10 years under the Company Directors Disqualification Act 1986 for engaging in fraudulent trading.

However, he decided to continue to pursue his fraudulent business and, in order to avoid the consequences of the disqualification order, he arranged for his sons, Ham and Ive, to register a new company, Just Ltd, with them as the only shareholders and directors of the company.

As neither Ham nor Ive have any business experience Ger arranged for his accountant Kim to run the business on his instructions. Although Kim took no shares in the company, and was never officially appointed as a director, he assumed the title of managing director.

Lyn, a customer of Just Ltd, suffered considerable loss on account of its fraudulent activity.

Required:

(a)   **Explain the potential liability of Ger, Ham, Ive and Kim for fraudulent trading.**(4 marks)

(b)   **Assuming that Ger is criminally liable for breach of a disqualification order, state whether Ger, Ham, Ive and Kim are personally liable for the debts of Just Ltd.** (2 marks)

(6 marks)

Question 36 FAY, GUS & HET

In 2014 Fay, Gus and Het formed a private limited company, FGH Ltd, to carry out technological research. They each took 100 shares in the company and each of them became a director in the company.

In January 2016 Fay admitted that she had been working with a much larger rival company, Ix plc, and that she had passed on some of FGH Ltd's research results to Ix plc in return for substantial payment.

Fay maintains that she has done no harm, as FGH Ltd was not capable of using the information. Gus and Het are extremely angered by Fay's actions and want to remove her as a director.

Required:

(a)   State the duty of a director to avoid a conflict of interest.   (2 marks)

(b)   Explain the requirements for removing Fay as a director of a private limited company.
                                                                                            (4 marks)

                                                                                    (6 marks)

Question 37 DIX PLC

Cy is a member of the board of directors of Dix plc, a construction company.

He also has a significant shareholding in Fox Ltd, a company specialising in supplying building materials. Last year Dix plc entered into a contract to buy a large consignment of concrete from Fox Ltd. Cy attended the board meeting which approved the contract and voted in favour of it, without revealing any link with Fox Ltd. The contract price was substantially above the market price and Fox Ltd made a considerable profit on the contract.

Required:

(a)   Explain whether Cy has breached any of his directors' duties.   (4 marks)

(b)   State Cy's liability to Dix plc.   (2 marks)

                                                                                    (6 marks)

Question 38 IMP LTD

Gim and Hom formed an online supply company, IMP Ltd, in 2012 and have been its sole directors since then. The business has never made a profit and has only managed to carry on trading by using its £50,000 overdraft facility with Just Bank plc.

In January 2014, IMP Ltd entered into a large deal and by October 2014 it was obvious that it had lost £100,000 on the contract. Gim and Hom treated the loss as merely unfortunate and carried on trading. They ignored the limit on the agreed overdraft facility and delayed payments on other outstanding contracts. They justified their decision on the grounds that they could recover all their losses to date from the profits of a new contract. Unfortunately, the new contract lost an additional £100,000.

In February 2016 Gim and Hom applied to have IMP Ltd wound up, owing debts of £250,000.

The realisable value of the company's assets is £10,000.

Required:

(a)   Explain whether Gim and Hom will be liable for either of the following:

   (i)   fraudulent trading under s.213 Insolvency Act 1986;
   (ii)   wrongful trading under s.214 Insolvency Act 1986.   (4 marks)

(b)   State the potential consequences to Gim and Hom as a result of their actions.   (2 marks)

                                                                                    (6 marks)

Question 39 MAVI LTD

Mike is managing director of Mavi Ltd. While the company's finance director, Pat, was away on extended sick leave, Mike asked a friend, Jack, to prepare the company's financial statements. Both Pat and Jack are qualified accountants. Jack provided Mike with a draft of the financial statements and Mike asked Pat to check them upon her return from sick leave.

Before Pat completed her review, Jack's sister, Lucy saw a copy of the draft financial statements in his office. On seeing that they showed a substantial profit, Lucy purchased some shares from another shareholder.

Pat's review, when completed, shows that Jack had made significant accounting errors and that the company has made a small loss.

Lucy seeks to sue Jack for professional negligence.

Required:

(a)   **Describe the standard of care required of Jack in preparing the financial statements.**

(2 marks)

(b)   **Explain whether Jack owes a duty of care to Lucy.**   (2 marks)

(c)   **Explain whether Lucy has any right of action against Jack.**   (2 marks)

(6 marks)

Question 40 DEE, FI, GEE & KI

In 2012, Dee, Fi, Gee and Ki formed a private limited company to pursue chemical research. They each took 100 shares and each of them became a director. The articles of association stated that Dee, a qualified accountant, was to act as the company secretary for a period of five years, at a yearly salary of £24,000.

In May 2016, Fi, Gee and Ki discovered that Dee had passed on some research results to a rival company.

As a consequence, Fi, Gee and Ki propose the following measures:

(i)   to remove Dee from the board of directors;
(ii)   to dismiss Dee from her post as company secretary without any payment for the work she has already done.

Dee claims that she has a contract of employment by virtue of the articles of association and that she cannot be removed before the five-year period is completed.

Required:

(a)   **State how Dee may be removed from the board of directors.**   (2 marks)

(b)   **State whether Dee has a contract of employment by virtue of the articles of association.**

(2 marks)

(c)   **Explain what payment, if any, Dee would be able to claim if dismissed from the post of company secretary.**   (2 marks)

(6 marks)

Question 41 CHU

Chu, a suitably qualified person, was appointed as the company secretary of Do plc. Since his appointment, Chu has entered into the following contracts in the name of Do plc:

(i)   an agreement to hire a car from Far plc which Chu used for his own, non-business related purposes;

(ii)   an agreement with Gro plc to landscape the garden of his, Chu's, personal house.

The directors of Do plc have only recently become aware of these contracts and are concerned that Do plc may be liable for them.

Required:

(a)   **State the meaning of implied authority.**   (2 marks)

(b)   **Explain whether Do plc will be iiable under the two agreements entered into by Chu.**
                                                                                      (4 marks)

                                                                                      (6 marks)

Question 42 LOSS PLC

The net assets of Loss plc are less than half of the company's called-up share capital and reserves. The directors are about to convene an annual general meeting (AGM) and wish to know whether they can consider the "serious loss of capital" situation at this meeting.

Required:

(a)   **State the obligations of directors when the company has significant loss of capital.**
                                                                                      (3 marks)

(b)   **Explain whether the AGM is appropriate for consideration of the serious loss of capital.**
                                                                                      (3 marks)

                                                                                      (6 marks)

Question 43 EARL

Earl has been employed by Flash Ltd, for the past 20 years. During that time he has also invested in the company. Earl owns 5,000 £1 ordinary shares in Flash Ltd that are paid up to the extent of 75%. The debentures, to the value of £5,000, are secured by a fixed charge against the land on which Flash Ltd's factory is built.

In April it was announced that Flash Ltd was going into immediate insolvent liquidation, owing considerable amounts of money to trade creditors (trade payables). As a result of the suddenness of the decision to liquidate the company, none of the employees received their last month's wages. In Earl's case this amounted to £2,000.

Required:

(a)   **State Earl's rights to his unpaid wages.**   (2 marks)

(b)   **Explain Earl's rights and obligations in regard to his shareholding.**   (4 marks)

                                                                                      (6 marks)

Question 44 MAT, MARY & NORM

On the advice of his accountant, Mat registered a private limited company to conduct his small manufacturing business. One of the reasons for establishing the company was to avoid liability for potential losses. The initial shareholders of the company were Mat, his wife Mary, and her father Norm, who each took 1,000 shares with a nominal value of £1. The accountant explained that they did not have to pay the full nominal value of the shares immediately, so they each paid only 25 pence per share taken.

When the company was established it became apparent that it needed to borrow money from a bank to finance an expansion in production. To that end Oop Bank plc lent the company £20,000 secured by a fixed charge against the land Mat had previously transferred to the company, with an additional personal guarantee from Mat for any further debts owed by the company to the bank.

Unfortunately the business has not proved successful and Mat and the other shareholders have decided that it is better to liquidate the company rather than run up any more debts.

Required:

(a)   **State the implications for Oop Bank plc of the loan being secured by a fixed charge.**

(2 marks)

(b)   **Explain the rights of the various creditors and the potential liability of Mat, Mary and Norm.**

(4 marks)

(6 marks)

Question 45 JASON

Jason, a British national, has been living abroad for the last three years. Having returned to England he plans to buy a plot of land being auctioned by New Homes plc. He knows the company's managing director and offers him, personally, £10,000 cash to arrange that the plot be sold to him privately, not by auction. The director declines the offer and when the plot goes to auction Jason is outbid by another buyer.

Required:

(a)   **State whether criminal or civil action, or both, can be taken in relation to bribery.**

(2 marks)

(b)   **Explain whether any criminal offences relating to bribery have been committed by Jason.**

(2 marks)

(c)   **Explain the liabilities of the managing director if he had accepted the offer and arranged for a private sale.**

(2 marks)

(6 marks)

Question 46 LARGE PLC

In January the board of directors of Huge plc decided to make a takeover bid for Large plc. After the decision was taken, but before it is announced, the following chain of events occurred:

(i)   Slye a director of Huge plc bought shares in Large plc;

(ii)   Slye told his friend Mate about the likelihood of the take-over and Mate bought shares in Large plc;

(iii)   at a dinner party Slye, without actually telling him about the take-over proposal, advised his brother Tim to buy shares in Large plc and Tim did so.

Required:

(a)   **State TWO offences of insider dealing.**   (2 marks)

(b)   **State on what basis Slye, Mate and Tim are guilty of insider dealing offences.**   (4 marks)

(6 marks)

Question 47 IAN

Ian is an accountant and one of his clients, Jet, runs an illegal operation as well as some other legitimate businesses. Jet approached Ian for advice as to how he should deal with the gains he makes from the illegal operation.

Ian suggested that Jet should use his legally made money to buy the local football club, Kickers, with the intention of passing his gains from the illegal operation through its accounts.

Ian reasoned that it would be easy to mingle the illegal money with the football club's legitimate receipts.

Jet accepted the proposal, bought the club, appointed Ian as its finance director and together they passed the illegal money through the football club. Lol, the long-term team manager of Kickers, has noticed the increase in the club's income, but is concerned that the extra money is going to Jet as the owner, and not being used to finance the club.

Required:

(a)   **State the TWO criminal offences associated with money laundering other than money laundering.**   (2 marks)

(b)   **Explain the liabilities of Ian and Jim under money laundering legislation.**   (4 marks)

(6 marks)

Question 48 JAZ PLC

Jaz plc is listed on the London Stock Exchange. Kip works for Jaz plc as an accountant. Whilst drawing up the annual accounts, Kip noticed that Jaz plc's profits were better than anyone could have expected. As a consequence of this knowledge, he bought shares in Jaz plc before its good results were announced. He made a substantial profit on the share dealing. Kip also told his friend Lu about the results before they were announced. Lu also bought shares in Jaz plc.

Required:

(a)   **State the definition of "insider" under criminal law.**   (2 marks)

(b)   **Explain the potential consequences to Kip and Lu if they are found guilty of insider dealing**.   (4 marks)

(6 marks)

MCQs 1 ENGLISH LEGAL SYSTEM

Item	Answer	Justification
1.1	A	The most accurate statement is that the aim of the criminal law is to regulate behaviour within society by the threat of punishment.
1.2	C	Insolvency law is considered to be private law.
1.3	A	In the ordinary sense means given their plain, literal, everyday meaning (the "literal rule"). However, it is the "golden rule" that ensures that the results is not absurd, inconsistent or repugnant.
1.4	C	Divisional court hears appeals of family law and appeals from county court on bankruptcy and land; many civil cases start in county courts.
1.5	D	Only the *ratio decidendi* is binding.
1.6	C	Literally "the reason for that which has been decided".
1.7	B	Prosecution and plaintiff are the terms used for the persons bringing a case.
1.8	A	(1) is a rule of statutory interpretation; (2) is a feature of common law.
1.9	C	Summary offences are tried by Magistrates; more serious offences are committed to Crown Court.
1.10	C	When signed by the Queen or her representative.
1.11	C	*Heydon's case (1584)* first recognised the "mischief rule" (judges should assume that legislation was introduced to cure an error or "mischief" in the pre-existing law, and should interpret the statute in line with that purpose.
1.12	B	A and C are not applicable.
1.13	C	£10,000 is the upper limit for claims within the small claims track with an exception for personal injury claims that have a limit of £1,000.
1.14	B	Appeal is to the Court of Appeal.
		Tutorial note: *The Crown Court deals with criminal law. The Supreme Court and Magistrates Court do not deal with appeals.)*
1.15	C	Not beyond *any* doubt. No case would be proved on that basis.
1.16	B	Directives require legislation in member states. Regulations pass into law automatically.
1.17	C	These are both accepted rules of statutory interpretation.
1.18	A	All other statements apply to the *obiter.*
1.19	A	EU Law takes precedence over domestic law; treaties made between the member states of the European Community are a primary source of European law.
1.20	C	The Administrative Court deals with administrative law matters and exercises jurisdiction over inferior courts; the Crown Court deals with criminal law.
1.21	B	The overriding objective is to deal with cases justly. The other objectives (e.g. fair and expeditious handling) contribute to that objective.

MCQs 2 TORT LAW

2.1	A	The reasonable person must have the same skill or expertise but not the same level of expertise (*Nettleship v Weston (1971)*).

2.2   D   As confirmed by the decision in the case.

2.3   A   *res ipsa loquitur* means the facts speak for themselves (*Ward v Tesco (1976)*).

            Tutorial note: *If the cause of the accident was not known there would be no fact to speak for itself.*

2.4   C   External and unforeseeable forces, independent of the event.

2.5   B   If personal injury is foreseeable to a foreseeable claimant, the defendant is liable for it even if some unusual weakness of the claimant's makes it worse than might have been expected.

2.6   D   Consequential economic loss that arises from damage or injury can be claimed in tort; damages are **not** available for purely economic loss.

            Tutorial note: *Loss caused by the acquisition of defective goods (C) is an example of purely economic loss.*

2.7   B   *ADT Ltd v BDO Binder Hamlyn (1995)*.

            Tutorial note: *The "special relationship" is considered outside the client relationship (so not C).*

2.8   A   Effectively, vicarious liability arises from a relationship between business partners or between a principal and agent.

2.9   A   *Volenti non fit injuria* means "to a willing party (i.e. consenting) no injury is done". This arises where an injured party willing exposes themselves to hazard (i.e. assumes risk).

2.10   C   A claimant's own negligence in causing the loss reduces his damages in proportion the blame.

2.11   B   A person who has no choice cannot be said to have consented so the defence of consent will fail. A person who assumes a known risk through compelling motives (e.g. to keep a job) is not giving free consent.

            Tutorial note: *Getting into a car with an inexperienced driver can be characterised as a situation of contributory negligence (along with failure to wear a seat belt).*

2.12   B   *Sayers v Harlow UDC (1958)*.

2.13   B   The "but for" test must be satisfied.

            Tutorial note: *A loss that would have occurred regardless of the negligent act is not a direct consequence of negligence (so the defendant is not liable). If a new intervening cause (novus actus interveniens) breaks the chain of causation the loss will be too remote (and the defendant will not be liable for it).*

2.14   A   *Volenti non fit injuria* would apply.

   Tutorial note: *However, if the girl had fallen over the barrier, rather than the teddy bear, Michael's rescue attempt would not have amounted to giving free consent.*

2.15   D   The main element is proximity but some likelihood of damage must have been foreseeable.

2.16   B   Under the "eggshell skull rule" Gerry *will* be liable (i.e. even though he could not foresee Tom's weakness making the consequences of the injury worse).

   Tutorial note: *Tom's disorder was not a new intervention because he clearly already suffered from it.*

2.17   A   The "reasonable man" is not a careless driver but has a duty to protect his own safety and the safety of others.

   Tutorial note: *The defence does not eliminate a duty of care. In Nettleship v Weston (1971) the defence of volenti did not apply because checking the insurance cover demonstrated that the instructor did not waive any rights to compensation*

2.18   B   For example, in *Sayers v Harlow UDC (1958)*, damages were reduced by 25%.

2.19   A   The auditor's *contractual* relationship is with the company. Only the company may sue its auditor for a breach of the duty of care.

2.20   D   A claimant must establish all three elements of negligence; that the defendant in question owed them a duty of care, that the defendant breached the duty owed and that the claimant's loss would not have occurred but for the breach of duty.

MCQs 3 ELEMENTS OF CONTRACT LAW

3.1   C   Setting conditions is a counter-offer.

3.2   A   The advertisement is an invitation to treat.

   Tutorial note: *Ann's offer is therefore an offer – not a counter-offer. Tee Ltd has no obligation to sell because there is no contract.*

3.3   C   30 July is when the acceptance is accessible to the offeror (even though he does not access it until 4 August).

3.4   B   *Hirachand Punamchand v Temple (1911)*

3.5   C   Acceptance is communicated when received by the offeror.

3.6   A   The letter of revocation is inoperative because it must reach the offeree before acceptance.

3.7   B   *Balfour v Balfour (1919).*

3.8   C   A minor can make contracts validly, so B is incorrect. A minor can repudiate contracts without liability unless the contracts are for necessaries, so C is correct and A is incorrect. D is incorrect because a minor would be liable to repay a loan even if he cancelled a loan contract.

   Tutorial note: *A minor may also have to pay interest on a loan as a reasonable price for the benefit received while the loan contract was in force.*

3.9   A   A price tag is an invitation to treat.

3.10   D   The car has been validly sold to Sophia.

3.11   A   A "binding in honour only" clause does not operate as a binding contract (*Jones v Vernons's Pools Ltd (1938)*). Agreements do not have to be in writing to have contractual force.

3.12   B   A simple contract can be oral as opposed to written (*parol*). Contracts must be supported by consideration, unless executed by deed.

3.13   D   The fall of the gavel ("going, going gone") is acceptance of the offer (bid).

3.14   B   All options other than B are social or domestic dealings that are presumed to lack intent to form legal relations.

3.15   A   *Byrne v Van Tienhoven (1880)*

3.16   D   Early payment of a smaller sum than due provides adequate consideration.

3.17   C   Like a reference letter it is not a binding promise.

MCQs 4 CONTRACT LAW – TERMS

4.1   A   The main effect of the Consumer Rights Act 2015 is that provisions purporting to exclude liability are **void** unless the party seeking to rely on them can establish that they are reasonable.

4.2   B   Condition terms are regarded as core terms of the contract. Innocent parties to the contact can repudiate any additional obligations owed by them if condition terms are broken and claim damages from the party which has breached the contract.

4.3   D   Consumer Rights Act 2015.

4.4   B   (3) is not correct as the innocent party will not have an option (i.e. be able to choose). Ability to terminate will depend on the serious of the effect of the breach of an innominate term.

4.5   A   Any ambiguities in the terms of the contract are construed in favour of the consumer.

4.6   B   Consumer Rights Act 2015 protects private customers in consumer sales. Since Ian clearly bought it for his business the exclusion clause is valid.

4.7   A   A contract which lacks some legally required formality is best described as unenforceable.

4.8   A   Clauses that exclude liability for negligence resulting in personal injury are invalid (CRA 2015).

4.9   C   If a warranty is broken the innocent party may claim damages for loss, but he does not get a right to repudiate.

4.10   C   A condition goes to the root of the contact and the injured party can claim damages (common law) and rescind (equity).

| 4.11 | C | This is **not** a common law ground for creation of an implied condition. |

| 4.12 | C | The claimant can walk away but is not compelled to do so the contract is not necessarily terminated. |

| 4.13 | A | F Ltd is not bound by the new terms without previous agreement to a change in the terms |

| 4.14 | B | Contracts of a continuing nature are voidable by minors. |

Tutorial note: *The contract is valid but as B is a minor he may avoid being bound by it without being liable for breach.*

| 4.15 | B | The contract exists and is valid but one party may not be bound by it (and therefore not liable for breach of contract). |

Tutorial note: *Although the law of misrepresentation is not examinable students should appreciate that such a contract is voidable rather than void (i.e. with no legal effect) or unenforceable (i.e. legitimate but lacking some required formality).*

| 4.16 | B | The Consumer Rights Act 2015. |

Tutorial note: *A term would have to be "unfair" to be not binding.*

| 4.17 | D | All three standards must be met. |

| 4.18 | D | The fairness test does not apply to all terms in consumer contracts nor does it apply only to exclusion clauses (so not A or B). Specifically, it does not apply to terms that specify the main subject matter or the price payable (so not C). However, the fairness test may apply even to these excluded terms if they are not sufficiently transparent or prominent. |

Tutorial note: *A trader must ensure that a written term of a consumer contract is legible and expressed in plain and intelligible language.*

MCQs 5 CONTRACT LAW – BREACH

| 5.1 | C | The injured party resulting from a breach of warranty may claim damages but not terminate the contract. |

| 5.2 | B | A contract can be rescinded for breach of condition but not warranty. Hence Den should not have rejected the goods and is therefore liable for having done so. |

| 5.3 | C | A condition is so central to a contract that its breach gives rise to both remedies. |

| 5.4 | D | A, B and C would be inequitable and/or unsupervisable. |

| 5.5 | B | Failure to comply with conditions (one pint bottles) entitled Mr Ramsbottom to rescission and damages. Thus the supplier has no grounds for a claim against him. |

| 5.6 | A | As established by common law. |

| 5.7 | A | This duty arises in claims in contract (and tort) and provides that an injured party cannot recover damages for any loss which could have been avoided by taking reasonable steps. |

5.8   A   Once the offer is accepted a contract comes into force.

5.9   B   Damages can never be punitive but only compensatory.

5.10   B   Damages are the established common law remedy for breach of contract and are available as a right.

        Tutorial note: *The other remedies given are equitable remedies that may be awarded at the court's discretion if damages are not suitable.*

5.11   A   As long as the estimate is genuine when the contract is entered into it will be valid even if the actual loss turns out to be less.

5.12   C   Breach of warranty entitles a claim for damages but not to repudiate the contract.

5.13   D   This equitable remedy is restitutory; putting the parties back to their original pre-contract position (e.g. allowing restitution of assets).

        Tutorial note: *B and C describe other equitable remedies of specific performance and quantum meruit, respectively.*

5.14   B   *White & Carter (Councils) Ltd v McGregor (1962)*

5.15   B   Part performance is no performance (except under certain circumstances). *Quantum meruit* is an award where damages are not available. However, it is Colin who is in breach of contract so he can have no claim.

        Tutorial note: *Inability to complete the contract due to unforeseen circumstances ("frustration") will only rarely be grounds for discharge of a contract (e.g. "acts of God"). Colin has no grounds (e.g. of poor health) to claim that he cannot complete the work.*

5.16   B   In *Hoenig v Isaacs (1952)* Hoenig was engaged to decorate Isaacs' flat for £750. He decorated the flat, but a wardrobe door and bookshelf were defective. Held: There was substantial performance and Hoenig was entitled to claim payment less the cost of remedying the defects (£56).

        Tutorial note: *If, however, the obligation under the contract is an entire one, even if there is substantial performance, it may not be possible to make a claim. For instance, if X agrees to paint Y's portrait and has painted everything except Y's eyes, it is unlikely that X would be able to make a claim.*

5.17   B   In the case of *Hochster v De La Tour (1853)* De La Tour engaged Hochster, in April, to act as his courier on his European tour, starting on 1 June. On 11 May De La Tour wrote to Hochster stating that he would no longer need his services. Hochster started proceedings for damages in breach of contract on 22 May. De La Tour claimed that there could be no cause of action until 1 June. Held: the plaintiff was entitled to start his action as soon as the anticipatory breach occurred (i.e. when De La Tour stated he would not need Hochster's services).

5.18   B   The claim is for liquidated damages.

5.19   A   Rose is contractually bound as she signed the order form. The car dealer has lost a sale. It has sold only one car where it would have sold two.

5.20	B	12 years applies to specialty contracts (under deed) and personal injury claims are limited to two years (*Limitation Act 1980*).
5.21	D	In construction contracts it is extremely difficult to measure damage, so the sum fixed will not unusually be a penalty.
5.22	A	Only liquidated damages apply (*Cellulose Acetate Silk Co Ltd v Widnes Foundry Ltd (1933)*).

MCQs 6 EMPLOYMENT LAW

6.1	C	The three tests are control test, integration test and economic reality test.
		Tutorial note: *Only two were listed. The "officious bystander test" relates to implied terms of a contract and the "fit and proper" test concerns professionals who conduct "relevant business" in the context of money laundering regulations.*
6.2	D	An employer's common law duty of care includes safe premises, equipment and system of work and competent staff. Although employers have a common law duty to comply with the law relating to working hours and provide rest periods and breaks this is not part of their common law duty of care.
6.3	C	(2) would suggest employee rather than independent contractor status.
6.4	C	It is a common law duty to pay for work done.
6.5	A	Colin has no claim as it is an employee's duty to obey a reasonable instruction.
6.6	A	The employer does not have a duty to provide employees with a reference.
		Tutorial note: *Under the Employment Rights Act 1996 (ERA) only employers who do not provide a written contract of employment are required to provide each employee with a written statement of employment particulars. This separate statement is not required if covered in a contract of employment.*
6.7	C	In the absence of a formal contract a statement of written particulars must be provided within two months.
6.8	B	This is a statutory requirement. One weeks' notice is only required for employees with up to two years of service.
		Tutorial note: *All employers (i.e. regardless of the number of employees) are required to comply with minimum wage requirements and provide detailed payslips. Although employers have a duty to provide a non-smoking workplace (as an aspect of health and safety) there is no legal requirement to cater for the needs of smokers.*
6.9	B	This occurs when both the method of dismissal and the reason for dismissal are inappropriate.
6.10	B	The statutory minimum notice period that Brian must give to his employer is one week. However, Brian is entitled to be given one week's notice for each of the 10 years of service he has given.
6.11	D	Generally, specific performance does not apply to service contracts.
6.12	C	The company must provide reasonable time off for these duties.
6.13	A	Vicarious liability applies to contracts **of** service, but not contracts **for** service.

6.14	D	Wrongful dismissal relates to breach of contract and is not constrained by age. It is also not time limited in respect of claims. However, compensation is capped by law.
6.15	C	The economic reality test looks at how the person is paid and who is responsible for income taxes.
6.16	B	Employment Rights Act 1996.
6.17	C	A settlement agreement is voluntary. It must be in writing. Although usually proposed by the employer it may be proposed by the employee. It can be offered at any stage of an employment relationship.
6.18	B	A "zero hours" contact is legitimate but "exclusivity" (as described) cannot be enforced (Small Business, Enterprise and Employment Act 2015).

Tutorial note: *A voidable contract is valid but one party may avoid being bound by it without being liable for breach.*

MCQs 7 AGENCY

7.1	D	Legal capacity is necessary for the contract to be formed.
7.2	B	*Watteau v Fenwick (1893)*
7.3	D	The letterhead is said to "hold out" the individual as having authority.
7.4	C	The doctrine of the undisclosed principal.
7.5	A	The capacity of the principal is relevant.
7.6	C	*Keighley Maxsted & Co v Durant (1901)*
7.7	C	The agent has the financial capacity of the principal.
7.8	A	It is the agent who should have disclosed that he was acting as agent.
7.9	D	Agents must obey only lawful instructions (*Cohen v Kittel (1889)*).
7.10	B	*John McCann & Co v Pow (1974)*. The agent must carry out the task personally or though his employees (*delegatus non potest delegare*).
7.11	D	Agency by necessity arises when a person in possession of another's property and unable to take the owner's instructions is obliged to do something with the asset to protect the owner's interests.
7.12	A	The managing director (or CEO, or Secretary) has implied authority (*Watteau v Fenwick (1893)*).
7.13	B	Actual authority may be express or implied.
7.14	B	This is where an agent is appointed to a certain position and the principal has impliedly agreed with them that they should do what a person holding the same position would usually do or be expected to do
7.15	C	Apparent authority arises when the principal represents ("holds out") to a third party that the agent has authority

MCQs 8 PARTNERSHIP

8.1 A A formal agreement is not a requirement for the partnership to be created.

8.2 A An incoming partner is only liable for debts incurred before his admission if he agrees to be so liable (so not B). The deceased partner's estate will be responsible for debts incurred before the partner's death (so not C).

Tutorial note: *However, a partner has implied authority for actions taken on behalf of the partnership.*

8.3 C Borrowing money (including a bank overdraft) requires actual authority of the other partners.

8.4 D Partnership Act 1890 (*s.10*), also Civil Liability (Contribution) Act 1978.

8.5 D As decided by common law.

8.6 B It operates as notice to all who have not dealt with the firm while he was a partner but knew him to be one.

Tutorial note: *There is no need to advertise to those who had no previous dealings with the firm and who did not know that he was a partner (obviously it is impossible to send notice).*

8.7 D Many partnerships operate without a formal agreement between the partners.

Tutorial note: *A partner may agree to be liable for debts incurred before they became a partner.*

8.8 D Unless the partnership agreement specifically provides otherwise a partnership is automatically dissolved on expiry of a fixed term or on the death (or bankruptcy) of a partner. On creation of a charging order (i.e. where a partner's share of the business is used as security for his own debts) the other partners can choose to dissolve the partnership.

Tutorial note: *Only the court may determine whether a partner has become permanently incapable of performing his part of the partnership contract.*

8.9 C This is the definition in the Partnership Act 1890 (*s.1*).

8.10 C Ted would be described as a sleeping partner because he is an investor in the business and shares profits but has no part in running the business.

Tutorial note: *A nominal partner simply lends his name to the firm. He does not contribute any capital, share in profits or participate in managing the business.*

8.11 A Dennis is no longer a partner and there is no express or implied agency and no question of ratification. No agency arises on the basis of Dennis holding himself out to be a partner.

8.12 B In the absence of an express provision, the Partnership Act 1890 provides for the right to share *equally* in profits and losses. There is an implied right of access to all partnership books and accounts.

8.13 B One person would **not** be sufficient. The requirement is for two or more persons to subscribe their names to the incorporation document.

8.14   A   In the absence of express provision, there is an implied right to share in the profits of the LLP equally. There is no statutory right to remuneration.

8.15   C   Peter and Paul have joint and several liability. The customer could assume Paul's implied authority *(Mercantile Credit Co Ltd v Garrod (1962))*.

MCQs 9 CORPORATIONS AND LEGAL PERSONALITY

9.1   A   The term "limited" applies to the members, not the company.

9.2   B   *Gilford Motor Co v Horne (1931)*.

9.3   B   This is a requirement of the Companies Act 2006 *(s.273)*.

9.4   A   Under certain circumstances, lifting the veil can expose sharcholders to personal liability.

9.5   D   (1) and (2) are both features of separate personality. (3) was decided in *Foss v Harbottle (1843)*.

    Tutorial note: *Although the Companies Act 2006 provides some exceptions to majority rule Foss v Harbottle is the general rule.*

9.6   B   There is no statutory minimum for a private company provided there is consideration for at least one share.

9.7   A   Only the company, as a separate legal person, can take action on behalf of the company.

9.8   B   The shares of a plc do not have to be quoted on the stock exchange.

9.9   D   Following *Macaura v Northern Assurance Co Ltd (1925)*, the company (as a separate legal entity) has the insurable interest and should insure its own assets.

9.10   D   A micro company has (1) a staff headcount of less than 10 and (2) a turnover **or** (3) balance sheet total not exceeding the micro business threshold. Howe Ltd meets all three criteria. Although Steve Ltd's turnover exceeds threshold for a micro business (£632,000) its balance sheet total meets the criteria of not more than £316,000.

MCQs 10 FORMATION OF A COMPANY

10.1   B   Confirmed by the suffix "Ltd".

10.2   D   Shelf companies are already formed and can commence operations almost immediately. The cost rarely exceeds £150. However, bespoke registration enables the founders to design the constitution to their needs.

10.3   A   The name of the company must be unique. The registered office can be changed.

10.4   D   The certificate of incorporation confirms the creation of the company, but a public company may not commence operations until it receives a trading certificate. This in turn is only issued on confirmation of the requisite capital requirements being fulfilled. Directors of a public company will be personally liable if the company defaults on debts for 21 days *(s.767)*. Private companies do not need a trading certificate and can therefore commence trading on receipt of a certificate of incorporation.

10.5   D   There is no limitation on the number of boards on which a director may serve (although under some circumstances it may create a conflict of interest and therefore breach the directors' duties).

10.6   D   The promoter is liable for the pre-incorporation contract (*Kelner v Baxter (1866)*).

   Tutorial note: *The company did not exist and therefore did not have contractual capacity when the contract was entered into.*

10.7   B   The word "Council" implies a connection with the public sector.

10.8   C   The investor becomes a member when registered by the company.

10.9   C   Pre-incorporation contracts bind those who enter into them, not the company.

10.10   B   A public company requires a trading certificate before commencing business so (1) is incorrect. An unlimited company can re-register as limited by a special resolution so (3) is also incorrect. (2) is the only correct statement.

10.11   D   Incorporation is achieved after the memorandum and articles are delivered to the Registrar of Companies.

10.12   D   A promoter does have legal liability for pre-incorporation contracts.

10.13   C   *Ultra vires* remains relevant but only in the context of members asserting their rights. It does not affect third parties.

   Tutorial note: *It is the members who can ratify an ultra vires transaction (s.239), not the directors.*

10.14   B   Transactions with third parties always stand, unless the third party had actual notice of any limitation.

10.15   C   Only company officers generally have a right to inspect the books of account (A) and minutes of board meetings (B). Anyone (not just members) may inspect the register of charges.

   Tutorial note: *Members are legally entitled to inspect minutes of general meetings.*

10.16   B   A person with significant control is an *individual* who ultimately owns or controls *more than 25%* of a company's shares or voting rights, or who otherwise exercises control over a company or its management.

MCQs 11 MEMORANDUM AND ARTICLES

11.1   A   A special resolution is always required, without exception.

11.2   C   The articles are the internal constitution and form a contract between the company and its members (and between the members).

11.3   C   A director can be removed by ordinary resolution with special notice.

11.4   D   The articles are a contract between the company and the members. However, not all directors of companies are members of the company.

11.5   D   A is incorrect, as a company can be formed by one person. B and C applied prior to the Companies Act 2006.

| 11.6 | A | Entrenched articles must be registered so that they will be identified by those searching the register. |

| 11.7 | C | The Memorandum is now a factual document, filed on formation and no longer alterable. |

| 11.8 | C | (1) is true (*Eley v Positive Government Security Life Assurance Company (1876)*). (2) is also true (*Re New British Iron Company (ex parte Beckwith) (1898)*). |

| 11.9 | D | Although *ultra vires*, the transaction is valid. However, the company may hold the directors personally accountable for exceeding their authority. |

| 11.10 | C | The Memorandum declares that the subscribers are forming a company and will take at least one share, or provide a guarantee. |

Tutorial note: *Statements of initial capital and proposed directors are part of the application for registration. An objects clause is not required.*

MCQs 12 SHARES

| 12.1 | C | Issued capital is the nominal ("par" or "book") value of shares allotted and paid-up capital is the amount paid to date by investors. |

Tutorial note: *Calculation questions will not feature in the F4 exam. Monetary amounts are included to provide an illustration for revision purposes only.*

| 12.2 | A | A company can be funded by loans and hold treasury shares. |

| 12.3 | C | Acquiring ownership of shares forms a contractual relationship with the company and members, bound by the articles of association. |

| 12.4 | D | None of the statements are correct. Non-voting ordinary shares and voting preference shares may be issued, as also may non-cumulative preference shares. |

| 12.5 | A | The subscribers are the founding members to whom shares are allotted on formation. |

Tutorial note: *They "subscribe" to the Memorandum of Association.*

| 12.6 | C | *Salomon v Salomon & Co Ltd (1897)* |

| 12.7 | B | A fraction of a share cannot exist. However, two or more people may jointly own shares (although the articles may put an upper limit on the number of joint holders). |

| 12.8 | A | Issued share capital is a nominal amount which does not reflect the value of the underlying net assets. The amount of cash paid is paid-up share capital. |

| 12.9 | B | Ordinary shares are not cumulative. A company cannot receive dividends on any treasury shares that it holds. |

| 12.10 | B | A poll (ballot) can be demanded by the Chairman or by any two members. |

MCQs 13 CAPITAL MAINTENANCE

13.1   B   Existing shareholders have a statutory right of pre-emption (*s.561* Companies Act 2006).

Tutorial note: *(1) cannot be a true as shares may be issued in exchange for shares.*

13.2   B   Subscriber shares of a public company must be paid for in cash.

13.3   B   Only a *public* company can make a public offer (so not A). Directors have the authority to allot shares (*s.549*)

13.4   D   *s.641* Companies Act 2006.

13.5   B   Five years is the statutory maximum (*s.551* Companies Act 2006).

Tutorial note: *The right to allot given to the directors can be revoked, varied or renewed at any time by ordinary resolution.*

13.6   C   Bonus shares are new shares issued to existing members, funded by reserves,

13.7   D   The share premium is the value paid less nominal value. Shares cannot be issued at a discount.

13.8   C   The account cannot be used to fund dividends at all, or to issue shares to new investors. However it can be used for bonus issues to existing members.

13.9   A   A scrip issue (also called "capitalisation" issue) is an issue of additional shares to shareholders in proportion to the shares already held (i.e. a bonus issue).

13.10   C   The purpose of issuing shares should be to raise capital (*Howard Smith Ltd v Ampol Petroleum Ltd (1974)*).

13.11   B   *s.641* Companies Act 2006.

13.12   D   The surplus must be realised (*s.830* Companies Act 2006). This is usually on the sale of the asset.

13.13   B   The articles prohibit and so must be changed. This could be effected immediately before the decision to reduce capital.

13.14   B   Clearly the creditors "buffer" will be reduced and hence the creditors may object to the court (*s.646*).

13.15   A   The statement is *made* by the directors to the members *(s.641)*. If the resolution is passed it must then be filed with the Registrar *(s.644)*.

13.16   C   Members will be liable to repay if they knew or ought to have known that the payment was excessive *(s.847)*. The directors are then jointly and severally liable for amounts not recovered.

MCQs 14 LOAN CAPITAL

14.1   C   The fixed charge is attached to a specific asset.

14.2   A   The same charges are ranked by date of creation.

14.3   B   A is not correct: If the company could not deal with the assets freely it could not trade. C is not correct: Charges (both fixed and floating) are registered with the Registrar at Companies House. There is no longer a requirement for a company to maintain a register of charges (i.e. it is not a statutory book) only evidence of registrable charges.

14.4   C   *s.860* Companies Act 2006.

14.5   A   The company creating the charge must register it within 21 days. If a charge is not duly registered it is repayable immediately.

        Tutorial note: *A charge-holder can apply to register the charge if the company fails to do so. Only a floating charge is voidable (by the liquidator) in an insolvent winding-up.*

14.6   B   All fixed charges rank before floating charges; then the charges are ranked by the date of creation.

14.7   C   21 days maximum.

14.8   D   The debenture is the written acknowledgement of the debt owed by the company. The other two documents are only binding on the members (and creditors are not members unless they own shares).

14.9   B   Date of creation of the charge.

14.10   C   Stock-in-trade continuously changes in value over time.

14.11   D   This is a statutory entitlement. Non-members may also make a "company search" for a nominal fee.

14.12   D   Crystallisation occurs in the event of default.

14.13   B   Although a floating charge over book is usual VVV Ltd does not have control over its book debts as the bank can apply cash received from major customers to reducing the amount it is owed. The charge is therefore fixed.

14.14   B   Generally accepted definition.

MCQs 15 DIRECTORS

15.1   B   The declaration should be made at the earliest opportunity.

15.2   B   *s.168* Companies Act 2006.

15.3   B   Members can only seek an injunction to prevent contracts being made in contravention of the company's constitution (i.e. before the contract is made). A right of veto would be impractical, as the shareholders would be acting retrospectively.

        Tutorial note: *Model articles of association do not limit the directors' exercise of the company's implied power to borrow money to support authorised activities.*

15.4   C   The board, acting collectively, are agents for the company.

15.5   C   The first directors are appointed by the members, but not necessarily at the first AGM. Private companies need not hold an AGM.

15.6   B   Directors have no automatic right to be paid for holding office. The articles of association usual provide for payment. Non-executive directors receive a fee, not a salary. In many small not-for-profit companies, directors are not paid at all.

Tutorial note: *By the statutory model articles directors' remuneration is fixed by ordinary resolution of the members.*

15.7   A   The company must notify the registrar of any change in the particulars of a director and date on which it occurred within 14 days (*s.167*).

15.8   B   The general duties of directors are to the company (*s.170*).

Tutorial note: *A majority of the directors may, however, bring a lawsuit against a director.*

15.9   B   The members can ratify the director's act (i.e. effectively "rubber-stamp" the action as legitimate).

15.10   A   Individual shareholders cannot hold directors to account as their claims are not foreseeable.

15.11   A   The board can, at its discretion, resolve to remove a director (e.g. in the event of his bankruptcy).

15.12   B   This is lower than the age of majority but coincides with the earliest school leaving age (*s.157* Companies Act 2006).

15.13   B   Public companies must have two directors.

15.14   A   *IDC v Cooley (1972)*

15.15   C   It is not unlawful to be a shadow director (i.e. a person who is not acknowledged to be a director) but the individual bears all the responsibilities of a director. Only the particulars of *de jure* (acknowledged in law) directors are registered with the registrar.

MCQs 16 OTHER COMPANY OFFICERS

16.1   C   Auditors have a contractual relationship with their audit clients. Their duty of care is to the company (i.e. the body of shareholders) and not individual shareholders. (*Caparo v Dickman (1990)*). Auditors, as experts, have a duty of care when giving advice in a professional relationship (i.e. when they know that it will be relied on).

16.2   D   Every company must keep accounting records in accordance with *s.386* Companies Act 2006. Accountability lies with the directors collectively.

16.3   A   C and D only apply to public companies. Many company secretaries are also directors. Unlike a director, a company secretary can be a corporate person.

16.4   C   A is the duty of the Chairman. B is a responsibility of a director.

16.5   B   A simple majority of the members can remove *(s.510)*. Special notice must be given. It is also necessary for a meeting to take place.

16.6   D   *Panorama Developments Ltd v Fidelis Furnishing Fabrics Ltd (1971)*

16.7   C   Option A is not a primary duty, though in the course of their work the auditors may detect fraud. Option B is impractical.

16.8   C   *s.498* Companies Act 2006.

16.9   D   All companies must include maintain records of (1) and (3). Since Cabbit Ltd deals in goods it must also prepare a statement of stock *(s.386)*.

16.10   A   A company secretary normally has the authority to deal with all administrative matters including employing staff. (The exact scope of his authority will usually depend on the size and nature of the company.) A company secretary does not normally have authority to deal with the purchase of property or borrowing.

16.11   A   The balance sheet is the minimum filing requirement for a micro company. A profit and loss account (and notes to the accounts) and reports of the directors and auditor are optional.

Tutorial note: *For a small company, only the auditor's report is optional.*

MCQs 17 COMPANY MEETINGS AND RESOLUTIONS

17.1   A   A name change requires a special resolution. A special resolution requires a special majority of 75% of votes cast by members who are present at the meeting (in person or by proxy) and entitled to vote.

17.2   D   The dissenting minority must be 15% (minimum).

Tutorial note: *Chris voted in favour of the resolution so cannot now object.*

17.3   B   Written resolutions apply only to private companies. They are passed by simple or 75% majority (as for resolutions in general meetings). Resolutions to dismiss directors and auditors cannot be written. Members require only 5% of the voting shares to propose a written resolution.

17.4   B   Only a simple majority is required *(s.168)*.

Tutorial note: *Even though only the simplest of calculations is needed (to determine that 501 is more than 50% of 1,000) there will **not** be such "numbers" questions in the F4 exam.*

17.5   A   Directors (and auditors) can be removed by ordinary resolution.

Tutorial note: *Special notice would be required also. A private company must convene a meeting to dismiss a director (also auditor).*

17.6   B   10% for a public company *(s.303)*.

17.7   D   The first AGM must be held within 18 months and thereafter at intervals not exceeding 15 months.

Tutorial note: *Notice may exceed 21 days (if specified in the articles) or waived (if all members agreed to a shorter period.*

17.8	B	For a public company, members with 5% of voting rights can request that a resolution be put on the agenda at the next Annual General Meeting.
17.9	A	General meetings that are not the AGM require a notice of 14 days.
17.10	B	This is the minimum under the Model Articles.

Tutorial note: *Any provision in the company's articles requiring a minimum of five or more members is **void**. Those holding 10% of the total voting rights may also demand a poll.*

17.11	C	The proxy attends the meeting effectively as an agent, but her actions will be outside the control of her principal.
17.12	A	All other matters require only an ordinary resolution.

Tutorial note: *Increasing the share capital of the company may be delegated to the board for up to 5 years.*

17.13	A	An ordinary resolution requires special notice (*s.511*). Also for removal of a director of the company (*s.168*).
17.14	B	Simple majority, but exactly 50% is insufficient.

MCQs 18 INSOLVENCY AND ADMINISTRATION

18.1	A	*s.239* Insolvency Act 1986.
18.2	A	Any directors who knew or ought to have known about impending insolvency may be liable.
18.3	B	Only the additional £5,000 borrowed after the charge was created is secured.
18.4	A	Neil is liable for the unpaid sum on his shares.

Tutorial note: *Again, calculations will not be required in the F4 exam.*

18.5	C	The liquidator may be nominated by the creditors at the creditors meeting or by the members (at a general meeting) if the creditors do not nominate.

Tutorial note: *The creditors will appoint another liquidator if the first-appointed liquidator cannot complete the winding up (e.g. dies or resigns).*

18.6	A	The Official Receiver is a public official who acts as provisional liquidator until a liquidator (insolvency practitioner) is appointed.
18.7	A	Creditors with *floating* charges over the whole, or substantially the whole, of the company's assets and undertaking are entitled to have the administrator of their choice appointed (Enterprise Act 2002).
18.8	B	*Ebrahimi v Westbourne Galleries (1973).*
18.9	D	Administration is not liquidation (winding-up) of the company. The aim of administration is to return the company to solvency. Although he can settle the claims of preferred creditors he cannot discharge liabilities to unsecured creditors (as this might compromise subsequent liquidation under the Enterprise Act 2002).

18.10   D   This may be implemented when the company is solvent.

18.11   D   The third grounds for a court appointment of an administrator is to obtain the approval of the creditors for a course of action to clear debts.

18.12   D   Grounds for a compulsorily winding-up include members passing a special resolution to seek compulsorily winding-up or a public company failing to obtain a trading certificate within one year of incorporation.

18.13   B   Only once all debts and charges have been paid, will the shareholders be entitled to a return of their capital and, if applicable, a share in any surplus assets.

Tutorial note: *Preference shareholders usually rank in priority to ordinary shareholders but do not get to share in surplus assets.*

18.14   A   B and D are the roles of a liquidator and C is the role of an administrator.

18.15   B   The fixed charge-holder's claim is attached to the collateral (i.e. assets that secure the charge).

18.16   D   Fixed charge-holders have first priority, but limited to the value of the collateral.

Tutorial note: *If a fixed charge-holder's (or preferential debtor's) claim is more that can be claimed, the balance may be claimed as an unsecured creditor.*

18.17   C   Typically, the order will be granted for 12 months, with the possibility of extension.

18.18   B   A pre-packaged administration ("pre-pack") sale is a pre-arranged sale of a business and its assets (**not** the company) on the commencement of administration.

18.19   A   For other types of winding up, the company is insolvent.

18.20   B   The insolvency practitioner is appointed by the Official Receiver.

18.21   A   The liquidator is treated as an officer of the company for liability purposes.

MCQs 19 FRAUDULENT AND CRIMINAL BEHAVIOUR

19.1   D   Wrongful trading does not have intent to defraud.

19.2   C   Jill may be personally liable. Wrongful trading is a civil offence (*s.214 Insolvency Act 1986).*

19.3   A   Wrongful trading arises when the directors continue to run an ailing company when they know, or ought to be aware, that it has no reasonable prospect of avoiding insolvent winding-up.

Tutorial note: *Fraudulent trading is a criminal offence and applies at all times (not only on winding up). It arises when any person (not just a director) is a knowing party to a company being run with the intention of defrauding the creditors.*

19.4   D   Directors have civil liability under the Insolvency Act 1986 for fraudulent trading (*s.213)* and wrongful trading (*s.214)* and criminal liability for fraudulent trading under the Companies Act 2006 (*s.993).*

| 19.5 | C | The Act recognises four offences: |

       (1)   Bribing another person (active bribery);
       (2)   Being bribed or seeking a bribe (passive bribery);
       (3)   Bribing a foreign public official; and
       (4)   Organisational failure to prevent bribery.

| 19.6 | D | Giving a bribe and corporate (organisational) failure to prevent bribery are two of the four offences under the Bribery Act 2010. |

| 19.7 | D | A person is "associated" with a commercial organisation if he performs services for the organisation or on its behalf (*s.8*). This is a wide definition that includes all these parties (as well as employees of the organisation). |

| 19.8 | A | One of the guiding principles in the prevention of bribery is top-level commitment to fostering a culture in which bribery is unacceptable. |

| 19.9 | B | Naming previous employees could contravene data protection laws. |

| 19.10 | B | Price sensitive information is inside information (i.e. not in the public domain). |

| 19.11 | B | The offence of fraudulent trading was created by the Insolvency Act 1986 but criminalised by the Companies Act 2006. |

Tutorial note: *Wrongful trading is a civil offence.*

| 19.12 | D | He has a defence to any money laundering allegation as he reported the matter to the MLRO. The offence of tipping off is committed when a disclosure is made to a third party that is likely to prejudice any resulting investigation. |

| 19.13 | C | Money laundering is concealing and disguising the proceeds of crime. |

| 19.14 | A | An agent has a duty to account for all monies received as a result of being an agent. |

Tutorial note: *On a matter of fraud the appropriate authority includes the Serious Fraud Office rather than the police.*

| 19.15 | A | Fraudulent trading is a criminal offence and it is not sufficient to show the officer "suspected" the company might not be able to pay its debts. |

| 19.16 | D | The offer is an offence (whether or not the offeree accepts the favour). Serious cases of bribery may be punished with an unlimited fine **and** imprisonment (up to 10 years). |

| 19.17 | A | A deferred prosecution agreement (DPA) is only available to companies, partnerships and unincorporated associations; it is not available to an individual. A DPA can only be proposed by a prosecutor where there is sufficient evidence to prosecute and it is in the public interest to propose a DPA rather than prosecute. |

Answer 1 BIZZY LTD

(a)   Standard of care

"Standard of care" describes the level, or degree, of carefulness that a person is required to display in a given situation. It is measured by what is "reasonable".

(b)   Dennis and Sam

As Bizzy would have known that Dennis was deaf he was owed a higher standard of care than other employees *(Paris v Stepney Borough Council (1951))*.

The same standard of care was owed to Sam as to other employees working on the building site. (This duty of care would include providing appropriate safety equipment, such as helmets, which workers were instructed to wear.)

(c)   A defence against negligence

Tutorial note: *Only one defence was required.*

Volenti non fit injuria ("to a willing party no wrong is done") is the defence of consent. Sam's failure to wear a safety helmet, contrary to instructions, was conduct that inferred his consent.

Contributory negligence is a partial defence under which Bizzy could argue that Sam contributed to the extent of the injuries he suffered.

Answer 2 PROFESSOR PARFITT

(a)   Duty of care

Under the "neighbour principle" a duty of care exists where:

(1)   The damage was reasonably foreseeable;

(2)   There was a relationship of proximity between the parties (i.e. the potential victim is of a reasonably foreseeable class); and

(3)   It is fair and just in the circumstances to impose a duty of care.

Tutorial note: *If all three tests are not satisfied, the claimant has no claim.*

(b)   Liability for loss of investment

As a professor in accounting Parfitt may be seen to be an expert. An expert owes a duty of care if he gives advice in a professional relationship (i.e. where there is proximity between the parties).

Parfitt would not be liable to Rusty because there is no relationship between them that would create a duty of care.

Parfitt would not be liable to Frank because, although there is proximity between them:

- he owed a duty of care as a lecturer – not as a financial investment expert;
- he did not offer advice;
- he could not have reasonably foreseen that Frank would reply on his statement.

Answer 3 GREGORY, DOUGLAS AND MICHAEL

(a) **Liability of Douglas to Gregory**

Douglas owed a duty of care to Gregory in the design of the storage tank. The design defect was a breach of that duty. The leakage should have been foreseeable by Douglas as a "reasonable man". Douglas is therefore liable for his negligent action.

(b) **Liability of Douglas to Michael**

With regard to the liability of Douglas to Michael, Douglas could assert the lack of proximity between himself and Michael. Douglas owed a duty of care to Gregory as the purchaser of the tank. It is not fair and just that Douglas could have foreseen that Michael's home would be harmed.

(c) **Liability for destruction of Michael's house**

Damages claimed must be the direct, foreseeable consequence of the Gregory's negligence. Gregory should have foreseen the potential hazard (of fire) arising from a petrol leak. He may argue that Michael having tried to light a barbeque in his garden constituted a *novus actus interveniens* (a new intervening cause). However, as Gregory's breach of his duty of care still remained (i.e. the land was still contaminated by the spillage) the "chain of causation" is unlikely to be broken *(Borealis AB v Geogas Trading SA (2010))*.

Tutorial note: *Michael did not act recklessly by trying to light a barbeque and so his action did not remove the effect of Gregory's breach of duty.*

Answer 4 ESCAPADE LTD

(a) **"Volenti non fit injuria"**

This means, "to a willing party no wrong is done"; that is, consent. Consent may be given expressly or inferred from conduct. Consent freely given (e.g. not under duress) is an absolute defence against a claim in tort.

(b) **Liability to Andrew for his injuries**

Escapade has a duty of care to any member of the general public who participates in its paintball games. The onus will be on Andrew to prove that Escapade breached that duty of care and that negligence occurred. Andrew may claim *res ipsa loquitor* ("the facts speak for themselves") – he would not have broken his arm if the fence had been erected securely.

Escapade may seek to rely on the defence of *volenti*. However, Andrew's consent was to the risk of serious bruising – not to the more serious injury of broken bones that he actually sustained.

Consequently Escapade will be liable to compensate Andrew for his injuries.

Answer 5 NETSCAPE LTD AND NETSCOPE LTD

(a)   **How "passing off" can arise**

Tutorial note: It arises where a person's reputation or commercial identity is misappropriated by another person, damaging or threatening the goodwill of the innocent party.

Passing off can arise through:

- falsely representing goods or services as being the goods and services of another person or business; or

- falsely holding out a business or its goods or services as having some association or connection with another business.

(a)   **Protection under tort**

"Passing off" seeks to prevent anyone from using a business name which is likely to divert business to them (*Ewing* v *Buttercup Margarine Company* (1917)).

It therefore protects the goodwill attached to particular business names (e.g. "Netscape").

Tutorial note: Mat is not prevented from using the same, or a very similar, name as another business under the business names requirements of the Companies Act 2006.

(c)   **Will Mat be liable**

Although Mat will not be prevented from registering his new company with the name of his choice he will be liable for an action for passing off, especially as he admits that his reason for selecting the name is an attempt to divert business from the existing business to his own new one.

Tutorial note: To bring a successful claim Netscape Ltd would have to establish (1) that goodwill or reputation attached to the goods or services of the business; (2) that the name Netscope would be likely to mislead the public; and (3) that loss or damage arose as a result.

Answer 6 HELEN & INGRID

(a)   **Application of contract law**

Helen and James

It is clear from the given facts that James, having agreed to buy the picture, has made a contract with Helen. Since Helen cannot complete the contract, she is in breach of it.

Helen is liable to compensate James for foreseeable loss. This is unlikely to be a monetary loss, but there might be some compensation payable for non-pecuniary loss (e.g. not being able to enjoy the picture). James would be expected to mitigate his loss (e.g. by seeking an alternative picture elsewhere).

(b) **Application of contract law**

Helen and Ingrid

Tutorial note: *If there is a contract, Ingrid will be liable to Helen in breach for having sold the picture to Kate. If there is no contract, Helen has no remedy. It is necessary to identify the separate stages of the negotiations between Helen and Ingrid to establish when, if at all, there was any direct, unequivocal acceptance by one of the women of an unequivocal offer by the other (Butler v Ex-Cell-O).*

The fact that Ingrid's circular went to a number of people does not in itself prevent its being the basis of a contract (*Carlill v Carbolic Smoke Ball*), but its wording suggests that it was merely an invitation to recipients to express interest (i.e. an invitation to treat).

The response to an invitation will be, at most, an offer. Ingrid's response, though, constitutes a rejection (*Hyde v Wrench*).

Helen neither offers nor accepts at this stage: she says that she will "think about it".

Tutorial note: *A promise to keep an offer open (an "option") is only binding where there is a separate contract to that effect and the offeree/promisee provides consideration for the promise to keep the offer open.*

When Helen finally says that she will take the picture for the original price, she is merely making an offer to buy at that price if the picture is still available. Ingrid is not in a position to accept the offer: the picture has been sold elsewhere. There is no contract (*Hyde v Wrench*).

Helen cannot acquire the picture, and therefore cannot complete her contract with James.

Answer 7 ALAN

(a) **Alan and Ben**

In commercial situations, there is a presumption that the parties intend to create legal relations.

Although they are son and father it is clear from the facts of the situation that they entered into a business relationship with regard to the provision of the accountancy services. Alan was to prepare the tax return for Ben's business and Ben was expected, and indeed agreed, to pay £500. In such circumstances there was a clear intention to create legal relations and Ben cannot avoid his liability to pay Alan on the basis of their familial relationship.

Tutorial note: *As with other presumptions, this one is open to rebuttal. In commercial situations, however, the presumption is so strong that it will usually take express wording to the contrary to avoid its operation.*

(b) **Dawn and Alan**

In domestic and social agreements, there is a presumption that the parties do **not** intend to create legal relations.

Dawn would appear to have no grounds to enforce Alan's promise to buy her the new car. The presumption against creating legal relations in domestic situations would be applied as there are no grounds for rebutting it (*Jones v Padavattan*).

Answer 8 AL & BASH CARS PLC

(a)   **Elements of contract law**

(i)   Invitation to treat

The original advertisement in the magazine was not an offer; it was merely an invitation to treat. As such it is not an offer to sell but merely an invitation to others to make offers.

Tutorial note: *The point of this is that the person extending the invitation is not bound to accept any offers made to them.*

(ii)   Offer

The first offer was made by Al when he wrote to both Bash Cars plc stating his terms of supply. Bash Cars plc was at liberty to accept Al's offer to supply the 1,000 filters at £50 each and thus enter into a binding contract (which Al would have had to perform or stand liable to pay damages for any breach of the contract).

Tutorial note: *The original letters Al received from Bash Cars plc was a request for information and did not amount to offers to purchase filters from Al (Harvey v Facey (1893)).*

(iii)   Counter-offer

(1)   Bash Cars plc did not accept the original offer, stating that it was only willing to pay £45 per filter. That letter amounted to a counter offer, which made Al the offeree rather than the offeror, as he had originally been.

(2)   Al's next letter restating his original terms represented a further counter-offer to the company's own counter-offer. That letters restored Al to his position as the offeror with Bash Cars reassuming the role of offeree, who could accept or reject the terms as it wished.

(b)   **Contract price**

The first counter-offer (£45) destroyed Al's original offer (£50), so that it could no longer be accepted (*Hyde v Wrench* (1840)) without further negotiations.

By sending the order for the filters, the purchasing director of Bash Cars accepted Al's counter-offer and therefore entered into a binding contract on Al's terms, which require the company to pay £50 per filter.

Answer 9 AMI

(a)   **Enforceable contract**

Common law provides that a person can only enforce a contract if he has given "consideration" for it (i.e. that he has given or done something of value in recognition of the promises to him under the contract). Cis was obliged under the original contract to perform the work and she performed the work. Therefore, she should have an enforceable contract with Ami.

(b)   **Performance of existing contractual duties constituting new promise**

A long-established rule of contract was that the mere performance of a contractual duty already owed to the promisor could not be consideration for a new promise (*Stilk* v *Myrick* (1809)).

The newer case of *Williams* v *Roffey Bros* (1991) expanded the rules. The Court of Appeal held that the hirer of a craftsman had enjoyed practical benefits (avoidance of a penalty) as a result of the craftsman's efforts, even though the craftsman did no more than he was contractually bound to do, and this was "sufficient" to entitle the craftsman to the extra pay.

Therefore, the performance of an existing contractual duty can amount to consideration for a new promise if there is no question of fraud or duress and practical benefits accrue to the promisor. Therefore, Cis has the right in law to enforce Ami to pay the extra consideration.

Answer 10 AMY & BEN

(a)   **Intention to create legal relations**

Domestic and social dealings

In domestic and social agreements, there is a presumption that the parties do not intend to create legal relations (*Balfour* v *Balfour* (1919)).

Tutorial note: *Similarly, in Jones v Padavatton (1969) a mother was held not to be liable to maintain an agreement to pay her daughter a promised allowance.*

Commercial dealings

The presumption is that the parties intend to their dealings to be legally binding. They can displace the presumption by making it clear that they do not intend to enforce the agreement by law (e.g. by including an exemption clause or clear disclaimer in the agreement).

(b)   **Amy and Ben**

The presumption in social dealings can be rebutted by the facts and circumstances of a particular case. If the parties' actions and intentions prove that they did intend their agreement to be binding, it will be enforceable. Although Amy and Ben are brother and sister they entered into an agreement about the website on a business basis.

It was not a domestic, family matter. Amy was to do the work for Ben's business and Ben was expected to, and indeed agreed to pay £1,000. In such circumstances the law will recognise a clear intention to create legal relations and Ben cannot avoid his liability to pay Amy. He may have wanted to help his sister, but he did so by entering into a business contract with her; one which she can enforce against him.

Answer 11 ADE

(a)   **Receipt of an offer**

Tutorial note: *An offer is a promise to be bound on particular terms, if the recipient (offeree) accepts. The offer contains the terms on which the offeror is willing to make a contract with the offeree. If the offeree accepts the terms, the result is a legally enforceable contract.*

Offers must be clear, complete and definite in order to provide the basis of an enforceable contract.

The advert was not an offer.

Ade has no claim against the auctioneers.

Tutorial note: *In turning up, Ade was merely following up the published statement of intention of the auctioneers to host the sale. The situation is similar to* Harris v Nickerson (1873), *in which the claimant was not able to recover damages for his costs in attending a cancelled auction.*

(b) **Option contract**

If an offeror promises to keep an offer open for a period of time, the promise is only binding if the parties make a separate contract to that effect, known as an "option" contract, supported by consideration.

If the offeree does not have an "option" the offeror can withdraw the offer at any time until the offeree accepts. Ade had not given Chip any consideration to keep the offer open and so the promise does not amount legally to an option to buy. Chip was within his rights to change his mind and break the promise. Ade has no rights against Chip.

Answer 12 ALI

(a) **Legal nature of Ali's advertisement**

Tutorial note: The issue to determine is whether Ali's advertisement was an offer or merely an invitation to treat. An offer is a promise that can be bound on particular terms. The offer may, through acceptance, result in a legally enforceable contract. It is important to distinguish an offer from other statements, which will not form the basis of an enforceable contract. In particular, an offer must be distinguished from an invitation to treat (i.e. an invitation to others to make offers).

Usually, newspaper or other public advertisements only amount to an invitation to treat and cannot be accepted to form a binding contract (*Partridge* v *Crittenden* (1968)). There are occasions, however, when an advert can amount to a genuine offer capable of acceptance by anyone to whom the offer is addressed (*Carlill* v *Carbolic Smoke Ball Co* (1893)).

The wording of Ali's advert was in such categorical terms that it might be seen to have been an offer to the whole world, stating his unreserved commitment to enter into a contract with the first person who accepted it. Ali would therefore be bound by acceptance of the offer.

(b) **Bud**

Tutorial note: Acceptance is necessary for the formation of a contract. Once the offeree accepts the terms offered, a contract comes into effect and both parties are bound. Acceptance may be in the form of express words, either spoken or written; or it may be implied from conduct.

The general rule requires that acceptance must be communicated to the offeror, although there are exceptions. One exception is acceptance through the postal service. In this situation acceptance is complete as soon as the letter, properly addressed and stamped, is posted (*Adams* v *Lindsell* (1818)). However, the postal rule will only apply where it is in the contemplation of the parties that the post will be used as the means of acceptance.

Tutorial note: Waiver of the offeror's right to receive communication is another exception to the general rule. However, this does not apply to Ali's advertisement (only to unilateral offers such as in the Carlill case).

Bud has clearly tried to accept the offer. However, he cannot rely on the postal rule to obtain the rug or damages, as the post was clearly an inappropriate mode of acceptance. There was only one rug on offer: it was implicit in the advert that to get it, you had to turn up at Ali's showroom. Therefore Bud has not entered into a binding contract with Ali.

Answer 13 ANO LTD

(a)   **Rules of consideration**

- It can be executed (i.e. performed *simultaneously*) or executory (i.e. performed in *future*).
- Past consideration is no consideration.
- It need not be adequate (i.e. "of equal worth") but must be sufficient.
- It must be lawful.
- It must move between the parties ("privity of contract").

(b)   **Additional payment**

Tutorial note: In order to require Ano Ltd to make the full payment, Box must show that he provided legally "sufficient" consideration for the new promise.

The performance of existing contractual duties is not consideration for a new promise *(Stilk v Myrick (1809))*.

In the case of *Williams* v *Roffey Bros* (1991), the Court of Appeal held that Roffey Bros had enjoyed practical benefits as a result of their promise to increase Williams' previously agreed payment for work under an existing contract (although Williams did no more than they were contractually bound to do).

Tutorial note: In this case the benefits were that the work would be completed on time, they would not have to pay any penalty and they would not suffer the bother and expense of getting someone else to complete the work.

Therefore, the performance of an existing contractual duty can be consideration for a new promise where there is no question of duress and practical benefits accrue to the promisor.

Box's situation is significantly different as he clearly exerted a form of economic duress on Ano Ltd to force the increase in the contract price. Ano Ltd was left with no real choice but to agree to Box's terms. Such unfair pressure would take the case outside of *Williams* v *Roffey Bros* and the old rule as stated in *Stilk* v *Myrick* would apply. Box would not be able to enforce the promise for the additional £1,000.

Answer 14 ABID

(a)   **Ways of including an exclusion clause in a contract**

Tutorial note: An exclusion clause can have no effect if it is not part of the contract, so it is necessary to determine whether or not an exclusion clause has been incorporated into a contract.

(i)   By notice

An exclusion clause will not be incorporated into a contract unless the party affected actually knew of it, or was given sufficient notice of it.

(ii)   By signature

If a person signs a contractual document, then they are bound by its terms, even if they did not read it (*L'Estrange* v *Graucob* (1934)).

Tutorial note: The only exception to this being where they were misled by the other party into signing the contract (Curtis v Chemical Cleaning & Dyeing Co (1951)).

(iii)   By custom

Where parties have had previous dealings on the basis of an exclusion clause, that clause may be incorporated into later contracts (*Spurling* v *Bradshaw* (1956)). However, previous signing of a document containing the exclusion is not sufficient to incorporate it into later contracts (*Hollier* v *Rambler* (1972)).

Tutorial note: *Only TWO of the above were asked for*

(b)   Reliance on an exclusion clause

Customarily, Abid did sign a contract in which the exclusion clause was clearly highlighted.

Although it is not certain whether Abid was actually aware of the content of the contracts he signed, it is likely that Bust Ltd can claim that the exclusion clause was incorporated into the contract.

Tutorial note: *Bust Ltd cannot claim inclusion of the exclusion clause by notice as Abid was not asked to sign the usual document. As a consequence Bust Ltd cannot claim inclusion by signature.*

(c)   Impact of the Consumer Rights Act 2015

Consumer Rights Act 2015 provides that exemption clauses that exclude liability for negligence resulting in death or injury are **invalid**. Therefore Bust Ltd cannot avoid responsibility for the injury sustained by Abid and will be liable for the injuries he suffered as a result of the negligence of the mechanic.

Answer 15 ANDRE

(a)   Remedies against Bath for the failure to provide a pool of the required depth

The usual remedy in cases of breach of contract is the payment of damages, to put the injured party into the position he would have enjoyed had the contract not been broken.

In cases where the common law remedy of damages would be inadequate the courts have discretion to award the equitable remedy of specific performance (i.e. an order that the party who is in breach actually carries out what he contracted to do). This remedy would be appropriate, for example, in a contract to sell a unique item which cannot be sourced elsewhere.

However, specific performance will not be granted where the court cannot supervise its enforcement as in cases of contracts of employment or personal service (*Ryan* v *Mutual Tontine Westminster Chambers Association* (1893)).

Andre will not be able to force Bath to carry out remedial work; his only remedy will be damages.

(b)   Remedies against Bath for failure to provide the correct filter system

Bath will not be liable for Andre's loss of a contract, as that did not arise directly as a consequence of the breach and Baths was unaware of it (*Victoria Laundry* v *Newman*).

Similarly, Bath should not be liable for Andre's allergic reaction (unless it was made aware of his particular predisposition when the contract was made).

Tutorial note: *Damages will only be awarded in respect of losses which arise in the natural course of things; or which both parties may reasonably be supposed to have contemplated, when the contract was made, as a probable result of its breach (Hadley v Baxendale (1845)).*

Answer 16 ARI, BI & CAS

Tutorial note: *This question asks candidates to analyse the problem in terms of the rules relating to the waiver of existing contractual rights.*

English law does not enforce gratuitous promises (unless they are made by deed). It only supports contracts in which there is consideration. This is also the case where a party promises to give up his rights under an existing contract, releasing the other from his obligations.

A principle, that a payment of a lesser sum cannot be any satisfaction for the whole, was originally stated in *Pinnel's case* (1602) and reaffirmed in *Foakes v Beer* (1884).

Tutorial note: *The rule was followed more recently in re Selectmove Ltd (1994) where a tax debtor was held to be liable to pay the full debt on demand from the tax authority, even though it had earlier agreed an instalment arrangement.*

On the face of it, it would therefore seem that Ari has a full claim against Bi and Cas. . However, there are a number of situations in which the rule in *Pinnel's* case does not apply.

(a) **Bi**

If the creditor agrees to take something other than money to settle a cash debt, the law will not look into the respective valuations and when the debtor makes the modified payment, the full debt is cleared. It should be noted, however, that in this context payment by cheque is not treated as being "different from" cash payment (*D & C Builders Ltd* v *Rees* (1966)).

Ari agreed to accept Bi's offer to do his accounts as payment of his outstanding debt. This constitutes payment in kind and there is nothing Ari can do to recover any more money.

(b) **Cas**

Where a third party intervenes to pay off an existing debt, but with a lesser sum, then the original creditor is not allowed to break their agreement with that party by going back against the original debtor for the balance (*Hirachand Punamchand v Temple(1911)*).

By accepting lesser payment from a third party (i.e. Cas's father), Ari can take no further action against Cas.

Tutorial note: *In the CBE exam all parts of Section B questions will be (2) or (4) marks. "3 + 3" marks questions may, however, feature in the paper-based examination.*

Answer 17 AZ LTD

(a) **Type of damages**

Damages defined in the contract terms are known as *liquidated damages.*

Such provisions will only be recognised by the court if they:

- satisfy statutory tests as to the fairness of contract terms; and
- are seen to be a genuine pre-estimate of likely loss foreseeable at the time the contract was made.

Tutorial note: *They are not intended to operate as a penalty against the party in breach. If the court considers the provision to be a penalty, it will not give it effect but will assess and award damages in the normal way (Dunlop Tyre Co v New Garage (1914)).*

(b)   **Claim for damages**

In *Azimut-Benetti SpA* v *Darrell Marcus Healey* (2010) the court upheld a very onerous liquidated damages clause which, as in this scenario, was triggered by termination of a ship building contract.   The court held that, on the facts of the case, it represented a commercially justifiable balance between the parties' interests.

Applying Azimut it can be concluded that, although the damages claimed appear extremely high, they are not punitive *per se* and are likely to be treated as a genuine contractual pre-estimate and so awarded by a court in any resultant court action.

Answer 18 APT LTD

(a)   **Nature of anticipatory breach**

There is clearly a binding contractual agreement between Apt Ltd and Bel, which Bel has stated she intends to break. This is an example of the operation of the doctrine of anticipatory breach.

The intention not to fulfil the contract can be either express or implied.

■   *Express* anticipatory breach occurs where a party actually states that they will not perform their contractual obligations (*Hochster v De La Tour* (1853)).

■   *Implied* anticipatory breach occurs where a party carries out some act which makes performance impossible (*Omnium Enterprises v Sutherland* (1919)).

As Bel has informed Apt Ltd that she will not be able to supply the manuscript before the due date of performance this amounts to *express* anticipatory breach.

Tutorial note: *This express repudiation of a contract is also called renunciation.*

(b)   **Response to anticipatory breach**

Since Bel's communication amount to an express anticipatory breach Apt Ltd has the right either to:

■   accept the repudiation immediately; or
■   affirm the contract and take action against Bel at the time for performance (*Vitol SA v Norelf Ltd* (1996)).

In either case, Bel is bound to complete her contractual promise or suffer the consequences of her breach of contract.

Answer 19 DAI & CHRIS

(a)   **Claim for unfair dismissal**

If an employee is dismissed improperly, there are a number of claims that might be open to him, including proceedings for unfair dismissal or for wrongful dismissal.

Chris had only been working with Dai for "a few weeks" and so he does not qualify to make a claim for unfair dismissal.

However, if Chris can show that Dai did not follow proper procedures in instructing him and in the dismissal itself, this may well constitute a breach of contract.

Tutorial note: *Even if Dai does not have a standard set of procedures, an employer owes his employee common law duties to provide appropriate training; ensure mutual co-operation and respect; and to give reasonable notice of termination – Dai may be seen to have failed here.*

On the other hand, Dai may be able to show that Chris failed to honour the employee's common law duty to do his job with reasonable competence, care and skill. However, although this may warrant the dismissal, it might not justify dismissal without notice.

(b)   Possibility of reinstatement

If Chris were to succeed in a claim, the available remedies will be limited to the amount which he would have earned if proper procedures had been followed. There is no right to reinstatement or to special damages unless these were part of his employment package.

Answer 20 FITZ

(a)   Distinction between contracts "of service" and "for services"

Tutorial note: *Employees are people working under a contract "of service". People who work under a contract "for services" are independent contractors. They are not employees, but are self-employed.*

It is essential to distinguish the two categories, because important legal consequences follow from the placing of a person in one or other of the categories.

For example, although employees are protected by various common law and statutory rights in relation to their employment, no such wide scale protection is offered to the self-employed.

Also ultimate liability for breach of contract or liability in tort depends on the person's status as an employee or self-employed.

(b)   Economic reality test

Tutorial note: *The economic reality test was first established in Ready Mixed Concrete (South East) Ltd v Minister of Pensions and National Insurance (1968).*

There are three conditions supporting the existence of a contract of employment:

(1)   the employee agrees to provide his own work and skill in return for a wage;
(2)   the employee agrees that he will be subject to a degree of control;
(3)   the other contract provisions are consistent with a contract of employment.

(c)   Application of economic reality test to Gus

It is more than likely that Gus would be treated as an employee. Both Gus and Hilda were described as self-employed but the label does not by itself define the relationship (*Market Investigations* v *Minister of Social Security* (1969)).

The manner in which they paid tax might indicate that they were self-employed, but the fact that Fitz provided them with their equipment suggests that they were employees.

The most significant factor would appear the degree to which Fitz controlled Gus.

Answer 21 DAN

(a) **Tests developed to distinguish the employee from the self employed**

The first test is the *control* test. In using this test the key element is the degree of control exercised by one party over the other.

The *integration* test shifted the emphasis from the degree of control exercised over an individual to the extent to which the individual was integrated into the business of their supposed employer.

The *economic reality* test is a multiple test that considers the employee's own work, the degree of control exercised over him and the consistency of provisions with a contract of employment.

Tutorial note: *Only two tests were asked for.*

(b) **Redundancy claim**

If an employment contract is deemed to exist, an individual can make a claim for redundancy on the basis that he was dismissed on the grounds that his skills were no longer required by the employer.

According to the tests in (a) above Eve was employed and may claim for redundancy. Fred, however, is unlikely to succeed in a claim for redundancy as he appears to be self-employed.

Employees who have been dismissed by way of redundancy are entitled to claim a redundancy payment from their former employer. Under the Employment Rights Act (ERA) 1996 the actual figures are calculated on the basis of the person's age, length of continuous service and weekly rate of pay subject to statutory maxima.

Tutorial note: *Calculations will **not** be required in the examination. However, by way of illustration, assuming that Eve is aged between 22 and 40 she will be entitled to one week's pay for each of her three years of service. As the maximum weekly cap is currently £479 she is therefore entitled to £1,437.*

Answer 22 GOAL LTD

(a) **Extending authority to individual directors**

There are three ways in which the power of the board of directors may be extended to individual directors.

(1) A director may be given *express authority* to enter into a particular transaction (or transactions of a particular type) on the company's behalf.

> **Tutorial note:** *Article 5 of the model articles allows the board to delegate powers to one or more directors. The company is bound by any contract entered into by the person to whom the power was delegated.*

(2) A director may have *implied authority* to bind the company in relation to matters that are usual, incidental or necessary to his particular position in the company.

> **Tutorial note:** *For example, a director acting as managing director or chief executive officer (CEO) would have implied authority to bind the company in matters consistent with the day to day running of the business.*

(3)   A director may bind his company is through the operation of *ostensible* (or *apparent) authority*, or agency by *estoppel*.

> **Tutorial note:**   *If a third party relies on this appearance of authority to do business with the company, the company will be estopped (barred in law) from denying that the person was authorised.*

(b)   Contract with Ima

Goal Ltd's name indicates that it is a private company and therefore the model articles apply. Hope does not appear to have been given *express* power to enter into the contract (and so the company cannot be made liable to Ima on this basis).

The contract might appear to fall within the implied authority of a CEO. However, Hope has not been actually appointed to that or any other executive post. Hope therefore does not have any *implied* authority (and Ima cannot make Goal Ltd liable on the contract).

However, the board of Goal Ltd has allowed Hope to act as CEO and to use that title. Goal Ltd is bound by contracts made by Hope within the scope of Hope's *apparent* authority as CEO (*Freeman and Lockyer* v *Buckhurst Park Properties (Mangal) Ltd* (1964)). Goal Ltd will be liable on this basis in the contract with Ima.

Answer 23 CHI, DI & FI

(a)   Liability of partners in an ordinary partnership

> **Tutorial note:** *Partnerships do not normally provide their members with limited liability, unless the partnership has been registered as a limited partnership under the Limited Partnerships Act 1907 or registered as a limited liability partnership under the Limited Liability Partnerships Act 2000.*

If an ordinary, unlimited partnership cannot pay its debts then the individual partners become personally liable. The Partnership Act 1890 (*s.9*) makes partners jointly liable for debts, and the Civil Liability Act 1978 provides that a judgement against one partner does not bar a subsequent action against the other partners. Only when the debts owed to outsiders have been dealt with, will the internal financial relationships be dealt with (according to the partnership agreement).

(b)   Liabilities of Chi and Di

> **Tutorial note:** *The partnership is clearly described as an "ordinary" partnership.*

> *(i)   Chi's unauthorised cash withdrawal from the bank*

Chi has clearly used her powers for an unauthorised purpose. However, the other partners cannot repudiate her transaction with the bank, even although it was outside her actual authority.

> **Tutorial note:** *This is because it is within his implied authority as a partner in a trading partnership to borrow money on the credit of the firm. The bank would be under no duty to investigate the purpose to which the loan was to be put.*

Chi will be personally liable to the other partners for the £10,000, by reason of her breach of duty to the firm. Her conduct may also constitute grounds for Chi and/or Di to have the firm dissolved.

(ii)   Di's purchase of books

Di's purchase of the books was clearly outside of the express provision of the partnership agreement to deal in works of art (as books are unlikely to be artworks). However, the partnership may be bound to honour the contract with the seller of the books (*s.5* PA 1890).

If the seller was not aware of the restriction on types of artwork to be sold (or if the books are works of art) then provided he understood Di to be acting in her capacity as a partner, the firm will be bound (*Mercantile Credit* v *Garrod* (1962)).

Tutorial note: *Within the firm, Di would be liable to the other members for her breach of duty and for any loss sustained in the transaction.*

Answer 24 GEO, HO & IO

(a)   Partners' liabilities for partnership debts

The facts indicate that this firm is an ordinary partnership, regulated by the Partnership Act 1890 (PA 1890). The liabilities of the partners are therefore unlimited.

Tutorial note: *If the debts of an ordinary partnership exceed the assets, partners' personal wealth may be called upon to pay off business debts. However, this is not the case in the given scenario.*

When a partnership is dissolved, partnership property is realised and the proceeds are applied according to the priority of creditors' claims.

If the assets are not enough to meet debts, partners' advances and capital repayments, then the deficiency has to be made good out of any profits held back from previous years, or out of partners' capital, or by the partners individually (in the proportion to which they were entitled to share in profits).

(b)   Meeting the creditors' claims

Tutorial note: *The priority of creditors' claims is as follows:*

- *to debts of outsiders;*
- *to any advances made by partners beyond their capital contribution;*
- *to capital contribution of the individual partners.*

*Any residue is divided between the partners in the same proportion as they shared in profits (s.44). But that is not relevant to this scenario. Calculations will **not** be required in the exam; this example is provided to illustrate the rules.*

Application to Geo, Ho & Io

As the partnership assets (£20,000) exceed the debts to outside creditors (£7,000), the creditors will be paid their debts in full.

Geo is entitled to receive repayment of his advance (£3,000) before any further distribution to the partners.

There is only £10,000 to distribute between the partners (£20,000 – £7,000 – £3,000). This means that the partnership has actually suffered a loss of £30,000 on the original capital contributed by the members.

The loss will be allocated, according to the partnership agreement, in proportion to the capital contribution. As the total capital contribution was £40,000:

- Geo, who provided £20,000, must suffer half of the loss ($^{20}/_{40}$);
- Ho, who provided £12,000, must suffer 30% of the loss ($^{12}/_{40}$); and
- Io, who provided £8,000, will suffer 20% of the loss ($^{8}/_{40}$).

In money terms the losses will be: £15,000 for Geo, £9,000 for Ho and £6,000 for Io.

Tutorial note: *In practice these losses will merely reduce the amount of capital returned to the partners. Thus Geo will receive £5,000, Ho will receive £3,000 and Io will receive £2,000.*

Answer 25 HAN, ITA & JO

(a)   Partner liability

Business assets must be used to pay the partnerships debts as for a registered company. However, unlike most registered limited companies, members of ordinary partnerships (i.e. formed under PA 1890) do not benefit from the advantage of limited liability and consequently their personal wealth may be called upon to pay off business debts.

Tutorial note: *Although the business name HIJ Potteries indicates that it is not a limited liability partnership the fact that it is an ordinary partnership is also clearly stated.*

The partnership agreement provides that Jo's liability for any business debts is fixed at £1,000 (her initial capital contribution). However, the partnership agreement is an internal document and its terms cannot bind outsiders without their express agreement. This means that outsiders can hold Jo liable for debts amounting to more than £1,000.

Tutorial note: *Jo would, however, be entitled to claim any additional sum paid over that amount from the other two partners.*

(b)   Order of distribution of partnership dissolution proceeds

Tutorial note: *Partnership property is only examinable in relation to the dissolution of a partnership and the order of the payment of debts.*

Upon dissolution, the value of the partnership property is realised and the proceeds are applied in the following order:

- to pay debts to outsiders;
- to repay to the partners any advances made to the firm beyond their capital contribution;
- to pay the capital contribution of the individual partners.

(c)   Partners contributions to partnership debts

HIJ Potteries' debts to third parties exceed assets by £4,000 (£9,000 – £5,000). The individual partners will therefore be personally liable for this amount.

The shortfall will be met according to the partnership agreement, which stated that all profits and losses were to be divided in proportion to the capital contribution. Han's advance of £1,000 to the partnership will be divided between the partners in the ratio of 6:3:1, as with the other losses.

Answer 26 FRANK

(a)   **Doctrine of separate personality**

When a company registers under the Companies Act 2006 it becomes a corporation, with its own distinct legal personality, completely separate from its members. This doctrine of separate personality applies equally to single person enterprises and to the largest of multi-national enterprises.

(b)   **Consequences of separate personality**

Companies have full contractual capacity in their own right.

Companies can sue and be sued in their own right.

So once a contract is entered into by a company, it is the company, rather than its individual members, which is liable for any default.

Tutorial note: *However, in some circumstances the courts will "lift the corporate veil" to look behind this separate identity.*

(b)   **Advice to Frank on the legality and outcome of his contract with George**

It is clear from the contract document that Frank entered into an agreement with the company George Ltd (not George the individual). He cannot, therefore, take action on the contract against George personally.

Tutorial note: *He might however be able to bring an action for breach of warranty of authority or for fraud.*

With regard to the contract itself, Frank will have to claim as an ordinary unsecured trade creditor of the company in its winding up.

Tutorial note: *However, the fact that it has gone into insolvent liquidation makes it unlikely that he will recover much, if anything, from the company.*

Answer 27 DOC

Tutorial note: *A company registered under the Companies Act 2006 is a corporation, a distinct legal person, with an identity of its own, separate from its members. The clearest expression of the doctrine is in the case of* Salomon v A Salomon & Co Ltd *(1897).*

(a)   **Dealings with Ed and Ed Ltd**

One consequence of the doctrine of separate personality is that companies have full contractual capacity in their own right. Once a company enters into a contract, it is the company, not its individual members, which is liable for any default.

Doc entered into an agreement with the company, Ed Ltd. Because Ed is not a party to the contract in law, Doc cannot take action against Ed personally.

Doc will have to claim as an ordinary unsecured trade creditor of Ed Co.

Tutorial note: *He will have to provide details to prove to the liquidator that he is a creditor. The liquidator will pay off the company's debts in a set order. Unsecured creditors are the last to be paid and in an insolvent winding up they are not likely to receive all, or any, of the money they are owed.*

(b) **Dealings with Fitt and Gen Ltd**

If a person misuses the doctrine of separate personality, the courts can enforce corporate liability against him and can enforce his personal obligations against the company and ignore the separate legal personality of the company.

In *Gilford Motor Co Ltd* v *Horne* (1933) a former employee tried to avoid a contract in restraint of trade by setting up and trading through a company. The Court of Appeal held that the company was a mere sham to conceal the defendant's breach of contract. The employee and his company were ordered to abide by the agreement he had entered into.

Following *Gilford*, it is likely that the court will ignore the separate personality of Gen Ltd and allow Doc to enforce the restraint of trade clause against Fitt.

Answer 28 DON

(a) **Binding contract before incorporation**

A pre-incorporation contract is a contract which a promoter enter into, naming the company as a party, before to the date of the certificate of incorporation and hence before the company's existence as a separate legal person.

Since a company cannot enter into a binding contract until it has become incorporated it is not bound by any contract made on its behalf before incorporation (even if it has taken some benefit under the contract).

Tutorial note: *The company cannot ratify the agreement even after it has become incorporated.*

(b) **The law relating to company promoters**

Whether a person is a promoter or not, is a matter of fact. The determining factor is whether the individual in question exercises some control over the *affairs* of the company both before and after it is formed up until the process of formation is completed.

As Don "was instrumental in forming Eden plc", it appears, that he assumed the role of a promoter and is subject to the rules that govern that position.

(i) *Sale of premises to Eden*

Tutorial note: *Don has clearly breached his fiduciary duty to Eden plc by making a secret profit from this contract with it.*

If the possibility still exists, Eden plc may rescind the contract. However it is more likely that Don would be required to reimburse the profit he made on the transaction to the company.

(ii) *Purchase of computer equipment*

Eden plc cannot be required to (and indeed cannot) be bound by the contract (*Kelner* v *Baxter*).

Consequently, the provider of the computer equipment cannot take any action against Eden plc (but will have recourse to action against Don for any losses suffered (*s.51* Companies Act 2006)).

Answer 29 FRED

(a)   Changing articles of association

The articles of association can be changed by special resolution (75%) of the members (*s.21* Companies Act 2006).

However, at common law the alteration has to be made "bona fide in the interest of the company as a whole". Those deciding the alteration must actually believe they are acting in the interest of the company, and the alteration must be beneficial.

(b)   Changing articles to force Fred to sell his shares

In *Dafen Tinplate Co Ltd* v *Llanelly Steel Co* (1907) a minority shareholder was acting to the detriment of the company. However, an alteration to the articles to allow for the compulsory purchase of any member's shares on request so to do, was held to be too wide to be in the interest of the company as a whole.

However, in *Sidebottom* v *Kershaw Leese & Co* (1920) an alteration to the articles to give the directors the power to require any shareholder who entered into competition with the company to sell their shares to nominees of the directors at a fair price was held to be valid.

As Fred is in direct competition with Glad Ltd, the alteration would be valid in line with the *Sidebottom* v *Kershaw Leese & Co* case. However, the actual alteration to the articles is wider than is necessary to cover Fred's situation (as it extends to all members, whether or not they are in competition with the company). Consequently, it is unlikely that the alteration would be validated by the court (*Dafen Tinplate Co Ltd* v *Llanelly Steel Co* (1907)).

Answer 30 GILT CO

(a)   Harry's facility fee

A director must not accept a benefit from a third party, which is conferred by reason of his being a director or his doing, or not doing anything as director (*s.176* Companies Act 2006).

Tutorial note: *In this context a third party is any person other than the company, an associated company or a person acting on behalf of the company or the associated company.*

There is no breach of duty if the benefit taken by the director is immaterial. However, the £50,000 paid to Harry is clearly material as it has induced him to use his influence as a director in contravention of his duties to Gilt Ltd.

(b)   Allotment of shares to Itt plc

The proper purpose for which the directors should allot new shares is to raise capital for the company. Any other purpose should be authorised by the members (in advance or by retrospective ratification). Any other purpose is an abuse of the directors' powers of allotment and a breach of their duty to act *bona fide* in the interests of the company (*Howard Smith* v *Ampol Petroleum* (1974)).

Tutorial note: *See also Hogg v Cramphorn (1966) and Bamford v Bamford (1969).*

Directors must not act in a way that restricts their discretion in making decisions that affect the operation of the company. The board of directors of Gilt Ltd contravenes the Companies Act 2006. The matter could be ratified by majority shareholders by a vote in general meeting (on which Itt plc would **not** be entitled to vote).

Tutorial note: If not ratified, the court can be asked to declare the share allocation invalid. Itt plc's use of those shares to vote in favour of the takeover bid would then also be invalid.

Answer 31 DEE & EFF

(a)   **Restrictions on distributions**

*Tutorial note: The Companies Act 2006 governs, and imposes restrictions on distributions made by public and private companies. It defines "distribution" as **any** payment, cash or otherwise, of a company's assets to its members other than specifically excluded matters such as the issue of bonus shares and the distribution of assets on winding up.*

Distributions must come from "profits available for that purpose" (*s.830*). These are defined as *accumulated realised profits less accumulated realised losses.* The profit or loss may be either revenue or capital in origin.

There are additional restrictions for a public limited company. Any distribution must not reduce the value of the company's net assets below the aggregate of its total called up share capital plus any undistributable reserves (*s.831*). This means that public companies have to account for "downward" changes in the value of their fixed assets ("impairments") in the determination of profits.

Fan plc had a distributable profit of £1,000 (realised profit £3,000 less losses brought forward £2,000). The distribution of £4,000 therefore contravenes the Companies Act 2006.

(b)   **Potential legal liabilities if dividend is paid**

Shareholders who receive a dividend that they know, or have reasonable grounds for knowing, was paid from capital, are liable to repay it to the company (*s.847*).

Therefore, since Dee and Eff should have known that the dividend was paid improperly they, at least, will have to repay the overpayment.

Tutorial note: Directors have a duty to use proper skill and care in recommending dividends. As Dee and Eff appear to have breached this duty they would also be personally liable to make good the difference to Fan plc for any part of the overpayment that cannot be recovered from the shareholders.

Answer 32 HOT LTD

(a)   **Types of security for loans to a company**

(i)   Fixed charge

A specific asset of the company is made subject to a charge in order to secure a debt. The company cannot dispose of it without the consent of the fixed charge-holders.

Tutorial note: The assets most commonly subject to a fixed charge are land and buildings.

(ii)   Floating charge

A floating charge is most commonly made in relation to the "undertaking and assets" and does not attach to any specific property as long as the company meets its loan obligations. The security is provided by the company's entire property, some of which may be continuously changing (e.g. stock-in-trade).

(b) **Order of priority**

Tutorial note: *Properly registered charges of the same type take priority according to their date of creation. However, fixed charge take priority over floating charges regardless of when they were created.*

As all three charges were properly registered the fixed charge takes precedence over the floating charges. Within each category, the charges take priority depending on date of creation rather than the date of registration.

Consequently, the charges assume the following priority:

(i) Ko-Bank's loan, secured by a fixed charge created on 5 April;

(ii) Ina's loan, secured by a floating charge created on 1 April;

(iii) Jo's loan, secured by a floating charge created on 3 April.

Answer 33 CLEAN LTD

(a) **When a conflict of interest may arise**

Tutorial note: *The Companies Act 2006 specifically deals with the duty to avoid conflicts of interest (s.175).*

A conflict of interest may, in particular, arise when a director makes personal use of information, property or opportunities belonging to the company. A conflict arises whether or not the company itself could have taken advantage of the property, information or opportunity.

(b) **Subsequent approval**

The board of directors can approve transactions in breach of s.175 (unless the company's articles provide otherwise). If the board does not, the members can condone the conflict.

Tutorial note: *Where conflicts are not approved, the director (or former director) can be made to account to the company for his benefits and profits.*

(b) **Action against Des**

Des has breached his statutory duty by allowing a conflict of interest to arise that he did not declare to the board (*s.177*). As he did not seek the approval of the other directors (or the members) he can be held liable to account to Clean Ltd for any profits he made on the transaction.

Tutorial note: *If Des tries to hide his personal profit behind the separate personality of Flush he will probably fail: the courts have power to lift the veil of incorporation where corporate identity is being used to mask personal liabilities (Gilford Motor Co v Horne (1933)).*

Answer 34 CAZ

(a)   Disclosure of relationship

Company directors owe fiduciary duties to their companies.

A director must avoid a situation where he has, or can have, a direct or indirect interest that conflicts, or may conflict, with the interests of the company (*s.175*).   Such conflicts are required to be approved by the board.

Directors have a duty to declare any interest they may have in a proposed company transaction (*s.177*).

Caz should have declared her interest at the board meeting and not voted on the contract (*s.182*).

(b)   Caz's liability

Caz did not declare her interest in either Era Ltd generally, or the particular contract in question.   Dull plc could have avoided the contract if it had found out earlier and acted sooner.   Caz can be held liable to account to Dull plc for any profit she made on the deal.   Caz will also be liable to prosecution and a fine (*s.183*).

Answer 35 JUST LTD

(a)   Potential liability for fraudulent trading

Tutorial note: *As the question scenario clearly states that Just Ltd was set up to run a fraudulent business and that Lyn suffered as a result of the fraud, it is unnecessary to pursue the issue of establishing fraud, as it can be taken as a given.*

Fraudulent trading is a criminal offence (*s.993* Companies Act 2006) which applies to any or all of Ger, Ham, Ive and Kim, as it appears that they have knowingly been parties to carrying on the company's business with intent to defraud creditors.

Tutorial note: *Ger is a shadow director; Kim is de facto a director.*

Ger, Ham, Ive and Kim will all be liable to contribute to the company's assets to pay off creditors such as Lyn, in the event of its being wound up under civil law and the Insolvency Act 1986 (*s.213*),.

Tutorial note: *s.213 IA86 does not only apply to directors, but to any person who has been party to the fraudulent trading, which clearly all four have.*

(b)   Personal liability of Ham, Ive and Kim

Tutorial note: *If Ger is liable to conviction and sentencing under criminal law he will also face potential civil liability.*

Ger will have personal liability for Just Ltd's debts for taking part in the management of a company while subject to a disqualification order (*s.15(1)* CDDA).

Ham, Ive and Kim are personally responsible (*s.15*) for the relevant debts of a company and jointly and severally liable for the debts for which Ger is liable.

Tutorial note: *Lyn could therefore be assured that the assets of Just Ltd and the personal wealth of Ger, Ham, Ive and Kim would be available to pay any debts owed by Just Ltd to her.*

Answer 36 FAY, GUS & HET

(a) Duty of a director to avoid a conflict of interest

Directors have a general duty to promote the success of their company (*s.172*). More specifically, a director must avoid a situation in which he has, or can have, a direct or indirect interest that conflicts, or may conflict, with the interests of the company. This provision "applies in particular to the exploitation of any property, information or opportunity (and it is immaterial whether the company could take advantage of the property, information or opportunity)".

(b) Requirements for removing a director

Directors can be removed at any time by a simple majority vote of the members (*s.168* CA). Gus and Het can therefore use their majority voting power to remove Fay from her role as company director of FGH Ltd. This applies even if the removal leads to a breach of Hay's service contract (*Southern Foundries Ltd* v *Shirlaw* (1940)).

Those proposing to remove the director (i.e. Gus and Het) must give the company 28 days' notice of the resolution. Fay must receive a copy of the resolution and is entitled to speak to the resolution at the meeting at which her removal is considered (*s.169*).

Answer 37 DIX PLC

(a) Duty to avoid conflict of interest

Directors have a general duty to avoid conflicts of interest under CA 2006 (*s.175*).

Other independent directors may authorise the conflict (*s.175*). The members of a company can also authorise conflicts which would otherwise be a breach of this duty (*s.180*).

Directors have a specific duty to declare any interest, direct or indirect, in any contracts, either proposed or already existing, with their companies (*s.177* and *s.182*).   It is a criminal offence, punishable by a fine, if a director fails to make the required declaration in relation to an existing contract (*s.183*).

A director's disclosure can take the form of a general declaration of interest in a particular company, which is considered sufficient to put the other directors on notice for the future (*s.185*).

Applying the above to the problem scenario, it appears that Cy did not declare his interest in either Fox Ltd generally, or the particular contract in question.

(b) Action against Cy and Cy's liability to Dix plc

Cy can be held liable to account to Dix plc for any profit he made on the deal. More significantly, he will be liable to account to Dix plc for its significant loss on the contract. Cy will also be liable to prosecution and a fine under CA 2006 (*s.183*).

Answer 38 IMP LTD

(a)   **Liability of Gim and Hom**

      (i)   *Fraudulent trading (s.213)*

      It is unlikely that there is sufficient evidence to substantiate a claim against Gim or Hom for fraudulent trading, as it seems they genuinely thought they could "trade their way" out of operational and financial difficulties. Although it has to be recognised that Gim and Hom did actually disguise the debts of the company, they did not do so in order to benefit themselves.

      (ii)   *Wrongful trading (s.214)*

      Wrongful trading does not involve dishonesty but, nonetheless, it still makes particular individuals potentially liable for the debts of their companies.

      It would appear that Gim and Hom are both certainly liable for an action for wrongful trading, because they carried on trading after it was clear that they ought to have known that there was no reasonable chance of the company avoiding insolvent liquidation.

(b)   **Potential consequences of actions to Gim and Hom**

      It is necessary to determine from which date Gim and Hom should be held responsible for the debts of the company. It is immediately apparent that there was no real prospect of the company avoiding insolvent liquidation as early as October 2014.

      Consequently, they will be personally liable for any debts accrued by the company after that date.

      They will also be liable to be disqualified from acting as company directors under the Company Directors Disqualification Act 1986.

      Tutorial note: *Directors may be disqualified from holding office for a period of up to 15 years under the provisions of the CDDA 1986 if they are found liable for either fraudulent or wrongful trading.*

Answer 39 MAVI LTD

(a)   **Standard of care**

      Standard of care is the degree of care expected of a person in order to discharge his duty of care to others. If a person does not show the appropriate standard of care, he is in breach of his duty of care through negligence.

      As a general rule a person's standard of care is measured by that of a "reasonable man" of equivalent position. The standard is higher in situations demanding special skills, or if the person discharging his duty has special knowledge, training or qualifications.

      In preparing the financial statements, Jack should have exhibited the standards of a qualified accountant and so should not have made significant accounting errors.

(b)   **Duty of care**

      A person owes a duty of care to his neighbours (i.e. persons who are so closely and directly affected by his actions that he should reasonably have them in mind if he considers the consequences of his actions).

Although Lucy is his sister, she is not a neighbour in this matter. Jack should not reasonably have had in mind that she could have been affected by any lack of care in preparing the financial statements.

(c) **Right of action**

Although Lucy may be able to show loss on the value of the shares purchased and Jack appears not to have met the appropriate standard of care, this is not enough. Liability in negligence is based on breach of the duty of care (*Caparo Industries plc v Dickman* (1990)).

Lucy has no right of action against Jack. She cannot bring a lawsuit in tort because Jack owed no duty of care to her, so he cannot be in breach of a duty to her.

Answer 40 DEE, FI, GEE & KI

(a) **Removing a board of director**

Directors can be removed at any time by a simple majority vote of the members (*s.168* CA06). Fi, Gee and Ki can, therefore, use their majority voting power to remove Dee from her role as company director.

Tutorial note: *All three must use their voting power to have a simple majority.*

(b) **Articles of association and contract of employment**

The articles of association constitute a contract between the members and the company (and vice versa). However, this contract only applies to membership rights. Dee can only enforce the articles against the company in her capacity as a member (*Eley* v *Positive Government Security Life Assurance Co* (1876)); not as a director or company secretary.

Since acting as the company secretary is clearly not a membership right, Dee would not normally be able to rely on the articles as the basis of the contract.

(c) **Claim for payment**

Tutorial note: *Although unclear the wording "without any payment" is unlikely to mean that Dee has not been paid anything for acting as company secretary, as she was appointed to that post four years ago on an annual salary.*

It is possible for the courts to imply a contract of service from the behaviour of the parties and rely on the articles to provide the actual terms of the contract (*Re New British Iron Co ex parte Beckwith* (1898)). Dee's claim suggests that she would seek payment that includes the unexpired period of her contract. However, she would only be able to claim payment on a *quantum meruit* basis (i.e. for the work done). Assuming that she is remunerated monthly this may only be £2,000.

Answer 41 CHU

(a) Implied authority

Implied authority derives from a person's particular position. It arises from the relationship which exists between the principal and the agent and from which it is assumed that the principal has given authority to the other person to enter into contractual relations as their agent.

Third parties are therefore entitled to assume that agents holding a particular position have all the powers which are usually provided to such an agent. Without actual knowledge to the contrary, they may safely assume that the agent has the usual authority which goes with their position (*Watteau* v *Fenwick* (1893)).

(b) Liability for contracts made by Chu

Tutorial note: *Although the old authorities (such as Houghton & Co v Northard Lowe & Wills (1928)) treated company secretaries as having very little authority to bind their companies, later cases have recognised the role of the company secretary as the company's chief administrative office.*

In *Panorama Developments Ltd* v *Fidelis Furnishing Fabrics Ltd* (1971), the Court of Appeal held that a company secretary was entitled to "sign contracts connected with the administrative side of a company's affairs".

(i) This contract is clearly in breach of Chu's authority, but the actual contract is within a company secretary's implied powers. Therefore, as long as Ex plc was unaware of his breach of duty (i.e. Chi did not disclose that the hire was for his personal use), Do plc will be liable on this contract as well.

(ii) In this case, Chu has not only clearly exceeded his actual authority, but has equally gone beyond his implied authority. Gro plc could not reasonably assume that Chu was acting as an agent for Do plc in commissioning the landscaping of his garden. Do plc will not be liable for the contract.

Answer 42 LOSS PLC

(a) Obligations of directors when there is significant loss of capital

The directors of a public company are required to hold a general meeting of the company if the amount of the company's net assets falls to 50 % or less of its called-up share capital (*s.656*).

This ensures that the financial difficulties that the company is facing is communicated to the shareholders and gives them the opportunity to discuss what steps should be taken.

The notice of the general meeting must go out within 28 days of any director's becoming aware of the shortfall, and the meeting must be held within 56 days of that discovery.

The directors are liable to a fine if they do not meet these requirements.

(b) **Appropriateness of the AGM**

Although an AGM is, by definition, a general meeting, the purpose of the meeting called to consider the asset shortfall, and the steps which may be taken, is very specific.

An AGM is convened to consider many "routine" matters (e.g. the annual financial statements, appointment of directors and auditors, etc) which would detract from the serious loss of capital.

Consideration of the asset shortfall at the AGM would therefore be inappropriate. No matter other than the asset shortfall may be discussed at a meeting convened for the purpose of discussing it.

There must therefore be two separate meetings.

Tutorial note: *The meetings could, of course, be held on the same day, and at the same venue, to follow one another. This would reduce the cost to the company of convening and accommodating the meetings and allow members to attend both meetings in one consecutive timeslot.*

Answer 43 EARL

Tutorial note: *Earl holds a number of concurrent relationships with Flash; as a member, as a creditor of the company (through his debenture holding), and an employee. As an employee and as a creditor he is owed money, which he will look to be repaid. As a member of the company with partly paid up shares he may be liable to contribute to the company's debts.*

(a) **Earl's unpaid wages**

Wages and accrued holiday pay are preferred debts (*s.175* Companies Act 2006 and Schedule 6 Insolvency Act 1986). However, the current limit is £800. For the balance of £1,200, Earl will have to claim against the company as an ordinary unsecured creditor.

(b) **Earl's partly paid-up shareholding**

The nominal value of a share normally fixes the amount which the shareholder is required to contribute to the assets of the company. Earl's liability, as a member, is limited to the amount (if any) remaining unpaid on their shares.

Tutorial note: *Shareholders must pay the full nominal value of any shares issued to them, plus any premium charged at the time of issue.*

Earl has only paid 75 pence per £1 nominal share. If Flash Ltd's assets are not sufficient to meet its liabilities in full, Earl is liable to contribute the amount remaining unpaid per share (i.e. a maximum of 25 pence per share, £1,250 in total) to the assets of the company.

Answer 44 MAT, MARY & NORM

(a) **Fixed charge**

A fixed charge allows the creditor (Oop Bank plc) to claim against a particular item of property (in this case, land) owned by the company issuing the charge. While the company is a going concern it cannot dispose of the property charged without the consent of the charge holder (i.e. Oop Bank plc). If the company breaches the loan agreement the creditor can have that asset sold to realise the amount of the claim.

Tutorial note: *In comparison, a floating charge, is a charge over a class of general assets and does not attach to any specific property as long as the company is meeting its obligations. In the event of a breach by the company, the charge "crystallises" and attaches to any assets of the general description that the company owns at that time.*

(b) **Rights of creditors**

If the land does not realise £20,000 Oop Bank plc will rank as an unsecured creditor for any balance from the company.

The shareholders have only partly paid for their shares. They will have to pay up the balance on their shares (£750 each) to go towards meeting the unsecured debts. If the company is insolvent and the unsecured creditors cannot be paid in full they will recover a proportion of the debt (a number of "pence per £1").

Mat has given a personal guarantee to Oop Bank plc and will therefore be personally liable to meet any shortfall after the bank has been paid as an unsecured creditor.

Tutorial note: *In the problem scenario Oop Bank held a fixed charge over land. The situation would have been different had its debt been secured by a floating charge. If the company's assets exceed £10,000 the liquidator must set aside "the prescribed part" towards meeting unsecured debts before a floating charge is paid off. The amount is set at 50% of the first £10,000 and 20% of any further assets, up to a maximum of £600,000.*

Answer 45 JASON

(a) **Criminal or civil action**

Under the Bribery Act 2010 (BA10), it is a *criminal* offence for a person or organisation (including a company) to seek, take, offer or give a bribe in a "relevant function or activity", which includes any activity connected with a business.

Civil actions can also be brought in the UK against both the giver and receiver of a bribe by the principal of a bribed agent, who has entered into a contract as a result of the bribe being paid to that agent.

Tutorial note: *It is important when reading the requirements of "Section B" questions to interpret whether to whether they relate to the scenario of "stand-alone". This part stated "in relation to bribery" (i.e. in general). Only parts (b) and (c) are specific to the scenario.*

(b) **Bribery offences**

Jason's offer of a bribe constitutes active bribery (as do promising and giving bribes); it does not matter that the director declined it.

Bribery is an offence under BA10 if it is committed anywhere (in or outside the UK) by a British citizen. Thus, it does not matter where Jason was when he offered the money to the director, he has committed an offence.

(c) **Liabilities**

A director must not accept a benefit from a person other than the company or its representatives in respect of his being a director or of his doing or not doing anything as a director *(s.176* Companies Act 2006). New Homes (or a member on behalf of the company) may bring an action against Jason for breach of duty *(s.260).*

The director would have committed the offence of passive bribery if he had accepted Jason's offer. (An individual who is found guilty of a bribery offence is liable to an unlimited fine and may be sent to prison for up to 10 years.)

As an agent of the company he would be liable to account for the cash he received (an unauthorised "secret" profit) and any loss arising on the sale (i.e. any shortfall on the private sale price as compared to the price expected at auction).

Tutorial note: Bear in mind that the fundamental duties of all directors (ss.171-176) may be relevant to questions in the syllabus area of corporate fraudulent and criminal behaviour. Other points that could have been mentioned here are the duty to avoid conflicts of interest (s.175) and the duty to declare an interest (s.177).

Answer 46 LARGE PLC

(a) **Offences of insider dealing**

Tutorial note: Dealing in shares, on the basis of access to unpublished price sensitive information, provides the basis for what is referred to as "insider dealing" and is governed by part V of the Criminal Justice Act 1993 (CJA).

An individual who has information as an insider will be guilty of an offence of insider dealing:

(1) if he deals in price-affected securities on the basis of that information;

(2) if he encourages another person to deal in price-affected securities in relation to that information.

(3) if he discloses it to anyone other than in the proper performance of his employment, office or profession.

Tutorial note: Only two offences were asked for.

(b) **Offences of Slye, Mate and Tim**

Slye is an "insider" as he receives inside information from his position as a director of Huge plc.

When Slye tells Mate about the likelihood of the take-over he commits the second offence of disclosing information that he possesses as an insider.

Mate then becomes an insider himself and so is guilty of insider dealing when he buys shares in Large plc.

When Slye advises Tim to buy shares in Large plc, he commits the third offence of encouraging another person to deal in price-affected securities.

Tim on the other hand has committed no offence. Although he bought shares in Large plc, he did not receive any specific information.

Answer 47 IAN

(a) **Criminal offenses associated with money laundering**

(i)   Failure to report

It is an offence for a person who is acting in the course of business in the regulated sector (e.g. an accountant) and who knows or suspects that another person is engaged in money laundering not to report the fact to the appropriate authority (*s.330*).

Tutorial note: *Failure to report is punishable by a maximum of five years imprisonment and/or a fine.*

(ii)   Tipping off

It is an offence to make a disclosure which is likely to prejudice any investigation under the Act (*s.333*).

Tutorial note: *Tipping off is punishable by a maximum of five years imprisonment and/or a fine.*

(b) **Ian and Jet**

It is clear that Ian and Jet are involved in money laundering. The original money to buy the football club was not the product of crime, so the purchase is not covered by the money laundering legislation. However, the club is being used to conceal the fact that the source of much of Jet's money is criminal activity.

Jet would therefore be guilty of money laundering (under *s.327* Proceeds of Crime Act).

Ian is also guilty of assisting Jet in his money laundering procedure. He is actively concealing and disguising criminal property (*s.327*) and his arrangement with Jet "facilitates the retention of criminal property" (*s.328*).

Ian is also liable for failing to disclose the suspiciously high profits from the football club (*s.330*) .

Lol should report his suspicions to the authorities.

Tutorial note: *In 2013 the National Crime Agency took over principal responsibility for policing money laundering in the UK.*

Answer 48 JAZ PLC

(a)   **Definition of an insider**

Insider dealing is governed by the Criminal Justice Act 1993. This defines an insider as a person who knows that they have inside information and knows that they have the information from an inside source (*s.57*). An inside source can be direct (e.g. having access to information by virtue of their employment or indirect (e.g. receiving information from an insider).

(b)   **Consequences of an insider dealing conviction**

On summary conviction, an individual found guilty of insider dealing is liable to a fine not exceeding the statutory maximum and/or a maximum of six months imprisonment. On indictment, the penalty is an unlimited fine and/or a maximum of seven years imprisonment.

There is also the possibility that the person who benefits from the information, which belongs to the company, will be required to account to it for any profit made. This would certainly be the case with regard to directors who engaged in insider dealing, as they would have breached their fiduciary duties.

Tutorial note: *"Summary conviction" is a conviction reached by a magistrate or court without the intervention of a jury; "on indictment" is before a jury.*

Therefore, as an employee of Jaz plc, Kip is an insider (*s.57*) and the information he has is certain to affect the price of the company's shares. When he buys the shares in Jaz plc he is therefore liable to a charge of insider dealing (*s.52*). Kip is also liable for the separate offence of disclosing the information to Lu other than in the proper performance of their employment (*s.57*).

As he received the information from an insider, Lu is treated as an insider (*s.57*) and is liable for trading on the basis of the information (*s.52*).

Tutorial note: *An exam question would focus on the nature of the offence rather than the consequences of the offence.*

Fundamentals Level – Skills Module

Corporate and Business Law (English)

Specimen Exam applicable from December 2014

Paper F4 (ENG)

Time allowed: 2 hours

This paper is divided into two sections:

Section A – ALL 45 questions are compulsory and MUST be attempted

Section B – ALL FIVE questions are compulsory and MUST be attempted

Do NOT open this paper until instructed by the supervisor.

You must NOT write in your answer booklet until instructed by the supervisor.

This question paper must not be removed from the examination hall.

The Association of Chartered Certified Accountants

Please use the space provided on the inside cover of the Candidate Answer Booklet to indicate your chosen answer to each multiple choice question.

1   Which of the following may imply terms into contracts?

   A   Statute
   B   Third parties
   C   The parties to the contract

   (1 mark)

2   There are a number of ways in which investors can take an interest in a company and such different interests have different rights attached to them.

   Which of the following NORMALLY participate in surplus capital?

   A   Preference shares
   B   Ordinary shares
   C   Debentures secured by a fixed charge
   D   Debentures secured by a floating charge

   (2 marks)

3   **In the context of the English legal system, which of the following courts ONLY has civil jurisdiction?**

   A   Magistrates' court
   B   County court
   C   High Court

   (1 mark)

4   **In the context of employment law, which of the following is an AUTOMATICALLY fair ground for dismissing an employee?**

   A   Unofficial industrial action
   B   Redundancy
   C   Refusal to join a trade union
   D   Legal prohibition

   (2 marks)

5   **Which of the following business forms does the use of the abbreviation 'Ltd' after the name of a business indicate?**

   A   A limited partnership
   B   A limited liability partnership
   C   A private limited company

   (1 mark)

6 Jas has been continuously employed for six years.

Which of the following states the minimum period of notice she is entitled to?

A One month
B Six weeks
C Three months

(1 mark)

7 **Which of the following is indicated by the abbreviation 'Ltd' at the end of a company's name?**

A The shares are not transferable
B The shares may not be offered to the public
C The shares are freely transferable on the stock exchange

(1 mark)

8 Section 122 Insolvency Act 1986 specifically provides a distinct ground for applying to have a company wound up on the ground that it is just and equitable to do so.

Which of the following parties may petition to have a company compulsorily wound up under that provision?

A Shareholders of the company
B Creditors of the company
C Debentureholders of the company
D The Secretary of State

(2 marks)

9 Mo has a significant holding in the shares of Nova Ltd. He wishes to use his shareholding to remove Owen from the board of directors but is not sure how to do so.

Which of the following must be used to remove a director from office?

A An ordinary resolution
B An ordinary resolution with special notice
C A special resolution
D A written resolution

(2 marks)

10 **A written ordinary resolution requires the approval of which of the following?**

A More than 50% of those actually voting
B More than 50% of those entitled to vote
C Unanimous approval of those entitled to vote

(1 mark)

11 Employment law is a mixture of common law and statutory provisions.

Which of the following is purely based on statute law?

A Summary dismissal
B Unfair dismissal
C Wrongful dismissal

(1 mark)

12 Jo's contract of employment states that she is employed in Glasgow. When her employer tells her that she has to work in London, some 500 miles away, Jo immediately resigns.

Which of the following may this be considered an example of?

A Unfair dismissal
B Constructive dismissal
C Summary dismissal

(1 mark)

13 **Which parties are bound by the terms of the tender when one party submits a tender?**

A The person submitting the tender
B The person requesting the tender
C Both parties
D Neither party

(2 marks)

14 **In the context of contract law, a bid at an auction is which of the following?**

A An invitation to treat
B An offer
C A counter-offer
D An acceptance

(2 marks)

15 Bee injured her eye after failing to close a safety gate on a machine as instructed. She was also not wearing mandatory safety goggles as required by her contract of employment.

Which of the following is this an example of?

A Novus actus interveniens
B Volenti non fit injuria
C Res ipsa loquitur
D Contributory negligence

(2 marks)

16 What is the effect of a finding of contributory negligence in the law of tort?

A It removes the requirement to pay damages
B It reverses the payment of damages
C It decreases the level of damages

(1 mark)

17 In the context of the English legal system, which of the following courts ONLY has criminal jurisdiction?

A Magistrates' court
B Crown Court
C County court

(1 mark)

18 Imran claims that Zak owes him £1,000 as a result of a breach of contract.

In which court will Imran start his action against Zak?

A The magistrates' court
B The county court
C The High Court

(1 mark)

19 In the context of case law, which of the following applies to an *obiter dictum*?

A It is binding on all future courts
B It is binding on all lower courts
C It is not binding on any courts
D It is not binding outside the court it was issued in

(2 marks)

20 Contributory negligence arises as a result of the fault of which of the following?

A The claimant
B The respondent
C A third party

(1 mark)

21 Ann got trapped in a public toilet due to the lock being faulty. Rather than wait for help, she tried to climb out of the window but fell and broke her leg.

Which of the following is this an example of?

A Res ipsa loquitur
B Volenti non fit injuria
C Novus actus interveniens
D Contributory negligence

(2 marks)

[P.T.O.

22 The law treats employees differently from the self-employed and has established a number of tests to distinguish between the two categories.

Which of the following is NOT a test for establishing an employment relationship?

A The subordinate test
B The control test
C The integration test
D The economic reality test

(2 marks)

23 Breach of which of the following terms does NOT allow the possibility of the aggrieved party terminating the contract?

A A condition
B A warranty
C An innominate term

(1 mark)

24 Which of the following, in the context of entering into a contract, constitutes a binding offer to sell a unique item of furniture?

A Placing an advert in a newspaper with a price attached
B Placing it on display inside a shop with a price attached
C Telling someone the price you may be willing to accept for it
D Telling someone you will reduce the marked price on it by 10%

(2 marks)

25 Mark has received the agenda for the annual general meeting of Rova Ltd, a company he has shares in. The agenda contains a number of resolutions to be proposed at the meeting, but being a new member Mark is not certain as to what is exactly involved.

In the context of company meetings, which of the following must be passed by a 75% majority to be effective?

A An ordinary resolution with special notice
B A special resolution
C A written resolution

(1 mark)

26 Section 122 Insolvency Act 1986 provides a number of distinct grounds for applying to have a company wound up on a compulsory basis.

Which of the following is NOT a ground for the compulsory winding up of a company under that provision?

A The company has not received a trading certificate within its first 12 months
B The company has not started trading within the first 12 months
C The company has suspended its business for 12 months
D The company has altered its primary business within the first 12 months

(2 marks)

27 Abe issued an invitation to tender for a contract and Bea submitted her terms.

Which of the following statements is accurate?

A   Abe made an offer which Bea accepted
B   Abe made an invitation to treat and Bea made an offer
C   Both Abe and Bea made invitations to treat
D   Abe made an offer and Bea made a counter-offer

(2 marks)

28 In the context of statutory interpretation, which of the following requires judges to consider the wrong which the legislation was intended to prevent?

A   The mischief rule
B   The literal rule
C   The golden rule

(1 mark)

29 It is not unusual for some company investments to carry cumulative dividend rights.

Which of the following statements about the declaration of cumulative dividends is correct?

A   They are not paid until profits reach a certain percentage
B   They are paid in the form of a bonus issue
C   They are paid out of capital
D   They are paid when profits are available for that purpose

(2 marks)

30 Which of the following statements in relation to effective consideration is correct?

A   It must be both adequate and sufficient
B   It must be adequate but need not be sufficient
C   It must be sufficient but need not be adequate

(1 mark)

31 In the context of the English legal system, which of the following defines the *ratio decidendi* of a judgement?

A   The decision in a previous case
B   The facts of the case
C   The legal reason for deciding the case
D   The future application of the case

(2 marks)

32 Dan has been accused of a criminal offence and is due to be tried soon. He denies responsibility, claiming that the prosecution has no evidence that he committed the offence in question.

Which of the following describes the standard of proof in a criminal case?

A On the balance of probability
B On the balance of certainty
C Beyond reasonable doubt
D Beyond evident doubt

(2 marks)

33 **Which of the following statements relating to limited liability partnerships is correct?**

A They are limited to a maximum of 20 members
B They must have a minimum of two members
C They must have at least one unlimited member

(1 mark)

34 Ho subscribed for some partly paid-up shares in Io Ltd. The company has not been successful and Ho has been told that when Io Ltd is liquidated, he will have to pay the amount remaining unpaid on his shares. However, he is not sure to whom such payment should be made.

In limited liability companies, shareholders are liable to which party for any unpaid capital?

A Creditors
B The directors
C The company
D The liquidator

(2 marks)

35 **Which of the following CANNOT petition for the compulsory winding up of a company on the grounds of INSOLVENCY under s.122 Insolvency Act 1986?**

A The board of directors
B The members of the company
C The company's creditors
D The Secretary of State

(2 marks)

36 Money laundering involves a number of phases in the overall procedure.

Which TWO of the following are recognised phases in money laundering?

(1) Relocation
(2) Layering
(3) Integration
(4) Distribution

A 1 and 2
B 1 and 4
C 2 and 3
D 3 and 4

(2 marks)

37 Which TWO of the following are AUTOMATICALLY unfair grounds for dismissing an employee?

(1) Engaging in trade union activity
(2) Constructive dismissal
(3) Dismissal on transfer of employment to a new undertaking
(4) Redundancy

A 1 and 2
B 2 and 3
C 3 and 4
D 1 and 3

(2 marks)

38 In the context of the law of agency, an agent will NOT be liable for a contract in which of the following instances?

A Where the agent fails to disclose that they are acting as such
B Where the agent intends to take the benefit of the contract and does not disclose they are acting as an agent
C Where the agent acts on their own behalf although claiming to be an agent

(1 mark)

39 The Employment Rights Act (ERA) 1996 sets out remedies in relation to unfair dismissal.

Which of the following is NOT a potential remedy for unfair dismissal under the ERA 1996?

A Reinstatement
B Re-engagement
C Re-employment

(1 mark)

40 **Which TWO statements are correct in relation to designated members in limited liability partnerships (LLPs)?**

(1) They must not take part in the day-to-day operation of the business
(2) They are responsible for filing the LLP's accounts
(3) They are fully liable for partnership debts
(4) They have limited liability

A 1 and 4
B 2 and 4
C 2 and 3
D 1 and 3

(2 marks)

41 The term insider dealing relates to a number of potential criminal offences.

Which TWO of the following are crimes in relation to insider dealing?

(1) Encouraging someone to engage in insider dealing
(2) Failing to report insider dealing
(3) Concealing insider dealing
(4) Passing on inside information

A 1 and 2
B 1 and 4
C 2 and 3
D 2 and 4

(2 marks)

42 **Which of the following can be accepted so as to form a binding contract?**

A A supply of information
B A statement of intent
C A quotation of price
D An agreement to enter into a future contract

(2 marks)

43 Contracts are legally enforceable agreements.

Which of the following statements regarding contractual agreements is true?

A They must be in writing
B They must be evidenced in writing
C They need not be in writing

(1 mark)

44 In relation to the law of negligence, a finding of *volenti non fit injuria* arises from the action of which of the following?

   A   The claimant
   B   The respondent
   C   A third party
   D   An unforeseeable event

(2 marks)

45 In the context of the law of contract, which **TWO** of the following statements in relation to a letter of comfort are correct?

   (1) It is a binding promise to pay a subsidiary company's future debts
   (2) It is a non-binding statement of present intention to pay a subsidiary company's future debts
   (3) It is issued by a parent company
   (4) It is issued by a parent company's bank

   A   1 and 3
   B   2 and 3
   C   2 and 4
   D   1 and 2

(2 marks)

(70 marks)

[P.T.O.

Section B – ALL FIVE questions are compulsory and MUST be attempted

1   Az Ltd operates a shipbuilding business which specialises in constructing and modifying ships to order. In 2011, Az Ltd entered into an agreement with Bob to completely rebuild a ship to Bob's specification for a total contract price of £7 million. However, after completion, Bob informed Az Ltd that, due to the downturn in the world economy, he no longer needed the ship. Az Ltd had already expended £5 million on altering the ship, and immediately started an action against Bob for breach of contract.

However, in the week before the case was to be decided in the court, Az Ltd sold the ship for the same amount of money which they would have received from Bob.

Required:

(a) State the purposes of awarding damages for breach of contract.   (2 marks)

(b) State the duty to mitigate losses.   (2 marks)

(c) State the level of damages Az Ltd can claim for breach of contract.   (2 marks)

(6 marks)

2   Clare, Dan and Eve formed a partnership 10 years ago, although Clare was a sleeping partner and never had anything to do with running the business. Last year Dan retired from the partnership. Eve has subsequently entered into two large contracts. The first one was with a longstanding customer, Greg, who had dealt with the partnership for some five years. The second contract was with a new customer, Hugh. Both believed that Dan was still a partner in the business. Both contracts have gone badly wrong, leaving the partnership owing £50,000 to both Greg and Hugh. Unfortunately the business assets will only cover the first £50,000 of the debt.

Required:

(a) State the liability of Clare as a sleeping partner.   (2 marks)

(b) Identify the liabilities of Dan as a retiring partner.   (2 marks)

(c) State from whom Greg can claim the outstanding debt.   (2 marks)

(6 marks)

3 Jon, who is 65 years of age, has just retired from his employment with a pension and a lump sum payment of £100,000. He is keen to invest his money but has absolutely no knowledge of business or investment. He does not wish to take any great risk with his investment but he would like to have a steady flow of income from it.

He has been advised that he can invest in the following range of securities:

(1) Preference shares
(2) Ordinary shares
(3) Debentures secured by a fixed charge
(4) Debentures secured by a floating charge.

Required:

In relation to the above investment forms:

(a) Identify which is the most secure. (2 marks)

(b) State which may have a cumulative right to dividends. (2 marks)

(c) State which NORMALLY participates in surplus capital. (2 marks)

(6 marks)

4 In 2008 Ger was disqualified from acting as a company director for a period of 10 years under the Company Directors Disqualification Act 1986 for engaging in fraudulent trading.

However, he decided to continue to pursue his fraudulent business and, in order to avoid the consequences of the disqualification order, he arranged for his accountant Kim to run the business on his instructions. Although Kim took no shares in the company, and was never officially appointed as a director, he nonetheless assumed the title of managing director.

Required:

(a) Identify which of the following categories of directors apply to Ger and Kim:

(i) *De facto*
(ii) *De jure*
(iii) Non-executive
(iv) Shadow. (4 marks)

(b) State the working relationship and duties of non-executive directors. (2 marks)

(6 marks)

5 Fran and Gram registered a private limited company, Ire Ltd, in January 2009, with each of them becoming a director of the company.

Although the company did manage to make a small profit in its first year of trading, it was never a great success and in its second year of trading it made a loss of £10,000.

At that time Fran said he thought the company should cease trading and be wound up. Gram, however, was insistent that the company would be profitable in the long term so they agreed to carry on the business, with Fran taking less of a part in the day-to-day management of the company, although retaining his position as a company director.

In the course of the next three years Gram falsified Ire Ltd's accounts to disguise the fact that the company had continued to suffer losses, until it became obvious that he could no longer hide the company's debts and that it would have to go into insolvent liquidation, with debts of £100,000.

Required:

(a) State whether criminal or civil action, or both, can be taken in relation to fraudulent trading and wrongful trading.

(2 marks)

(b) Explain whether Fran or Gram will be liable for either of the following:

(i) Fraudulent trading under s.213 Insolvency Act 1986;
(ii) Wrongful trading under s.214 Insolvency Act 1986.

(4 marks)

(6 marks)

End of Question Paper

14

Answers

Section A

1   A
2   B
3   B
4   A
5   C
6   B
7   B
8   A
9   B
10 A
11 B
12 B
13 A
14 B
15 B
16 C
17 B
18 B
19 C
20 A
21 D
22 A
23 B
24 D
25 B
26 D
27 B
28 A
29 D
30 C
31 C
32 C
33 B
34 C
35 B
36 C
37 D
38 A
39 C
40 B
41 B
42 C
43 C
44 A
45 B

Section B

1   (a)   Damages in contract are intended to compensate an injured party for any financial loss sustained as a consequence of another
           party's breach. The object is not to punish the party in breach, so the amount of damages awarded can never be greater than
           the actual loss suffered. The usual aim of the award of damages is to put the injured party in the same position they would
           have been in had the contract been properly performed (expectation loss).

    (b)   The duty to mitigate losses ensures that the injured party is under a duty to take all reasonable steps to minimise their loss.
           As a result, the seller of goods, which are not accepted, has not only to try to sell the goods to someone else but is also
           required to get as good a price as they can when they sell them (*Payzu* v *Saunders* (1919)). If goods are not delivered under
           a contract, the buyer is entitled to go into the market and buy similar goods, paying the market price prevailing at the time.
           They can then claim the difference in price between what they paid and the original contract price as damages.

(c) Applying the foregoing to the contract between Az Ltd and Bob, it can be seen that Az Ltd managed to recoup all of the costs and potential profit it would have made on the contract with Bob, so is not in a position to claim any further damages from Bob.

2 **(a)** Her status as a sleeping partner gives Clare no additional protection from the unlimited liability which applies to all ordinary partners in an ordinary partnership. It simply means she has left her personal wealth open to clams over which she has no practical control through her own inaction.

(b) He remains liable to *existing* customers until those customers are informed that he has left the partnership.

He also remains liable to *new* customers who knew he was a member of the partnership, unless he has made public his withdrawal.

(c) Greg can claim from all three parties: Clare, Dan and Eve.

3 **(a)** As loans, debentures are more secure than shares. Debentures secured by fixed charges are more secure than those secured by floating charges. Consequently, debentures secured by fixed charges are the most secure form of investment of those listed. They do, however, receive the least in terms of return.

(b) Of the four investment forms only shares receive dividends, as debentures receive interest due to the fact that they are forms of loan. Of the share forms only the preference share can carry a right to a cumulative dividend, as ordinary shares only get a return on the profits generated by the company in any particular year.

(c) Only shares have any claim against surplus capital, as debentures are only secured against the amount loaned.

Of the two types of shares, preference shares MAY have rights to enjoy access to surplus capital but ONLY ordinary shares have such facility as a right.

4 **(a)** Ger acts behind the scenes and is clearly operating as a shadow director. Kim has not been appointed as such but acts as a director, which makes him a *de facto* director.

(b) As with all directors, non-executives owe fiduciary duties (now stated in statute) to their company. They are also subject to all legal regulation applying to ordinary directors. They may attend company meetings and have full voting rights.

5 **(a)** Criminal liability is only applicable to fraudulent trading under the Companies Act 2006. However, civil action is open under ss.213 and 214 Insolvency Act 1986 in relation to both fraudulent and wrongful trading.

(b) As a consequence of his falsification of the accounts, Gram is potentially liable under s.213 Insolvency Act 1986 fraudulent trading provisions.

Fran, on the other hand, may not have been liable for fraud but is certainly liable for wrongful trading for not taking the appropriate action to prevent the subsequent losses sustained by the company.

Section A

1–45   One or two marks per question; total marks 70

Section B

1   **(a)**   1 mark for each relevant point made relating to damages up to the maximum 2 marks.

   (b)   1 mark for each relevant point made relating to the duty to mitigate losses, up to the maximum 2 marks.

   (c)   1 mark for correct application and 1 mark for explanation.

2   **(a)**   1 mark for each relevant point made relating to the potential liability of Clare as a sleeping partner, up to the maximum 2 marks.

   (b)   1 mark for each relevant point made relating to the potential liability of Dan as a retired partner, up to the maximum 2 marks.

   (c)   Full 2 marks only to be given to a fully correct answer.

   Partial answers to be limited to 1 mark.

3   **(a)**   1 mark for correct statement and 1 mark for explanation.

   (b)   1 mark for correct statement and 1 mark for explanation of cumulative rights.

   (c)   1 mark for correct statement and 1 mark for explanation of surplus capital.

4   **(a)**   3–4 marks for a complete explanation of the different types of director and a correct application to Ger and Kim.

   1–2 marks for some understanding but lacking either application or explanation.

   0 marks for no understanding of the substance of the question.

   (b)   1 mark for each relevant point made relating to the role/function of non-executive directors, up to the maximum 2 marks.

5   **(a)**   A full answer distinguishing between fraudulent and wrongful trading is required for both marks to be given.

   1 mark for any relevant point made relating to either action.

   (b)   4 marks for a full answer clearly distinguishing the two types of activity and correctly applying them.

   1 mark each for correctly stating how each provision will be applied to the parties.

   1 mark for any relevant point made relating to either party's action.

Corporate and Business Law (English)

Monday 8 December 2014

Time allowed: 2 hours

This paper is divided into two sections:

Section A – ALL 45 questions are compulsory and MUST be attempted

Section B – ALL FIVE questions are compulsory and MUST be attempted

Do NOT open this paper until instructed by the supervisor.

You must NOT write in your answer booklet until instructed by the supervisor.

This question paper must not be removed from the examination hall.

The Association of Chartered Certified Accountants

Please use the space provided on the inside cover of the Candidate Answer Booklet to indicate your chosen answer to each multiple choice question.

1   Which of the following involves an offer which may only be accepted by performing an action?

   A   A collateral contract
   B   A unilateral contract
   C   A bilateral contract

(1 mark)

2   An agency relationship which is made retrospectively is referred to by which of the following terms?

   A   Agency by estoppel
   B   Agency by ratification
   C   Agency by necessity

(1 mark)

3   In contract law, the 'market rule' arises in relation to which of the following?

   A   Offer
   B   Consideration
   C   Remoteness
   D   Mitigation

(2 marks)

4   In relation to a debenture, which of the following is NOT true?

   A   It may be issued at a discount
   B   Interest on it may be paid from capital
   C   It is paid after preference shares
   D   It is freely transferable

(2 marks)

5   Tan writes to Yun stating that he will sell his car to him for £10,000. At the same time, Yun writes to Tan stating that he will buy his car for £10,000.

   Which of the following statements applies to this situation?

   A   There is a binding agreement due to the postal rule
   B   There is a collateral contract
   C   There is neither an agreement nor a contract

(1 mark)

6 **Which of the following statements about contracts of employment is true?**

A They can be made either orally or in writing
B They must be made in writing
C They must be evidenced in writing

(1 mark)

7 **Where directors make a false statement of solvency prior to a members' voluntary liquidation, which of the following have they committed under the relevant legislation?**

A A breach of criminal law with criminal penalties
B A breach of civil law with criminal penalties
C A breach of civil law with civil liability
D A breach of both civil and criminal law with liabilities under both

(2 marks)

8 **Which of the following is the consequence when a patient signs a medical consent form before an operation?**

A The patient gives up any right of action for any injury suffered
B Any action for any injury suffered during the operation is limited to negligence
C The level of any potential payment for any injury suffered is reduced

(1 mark)

9 **Where a contract states the sum to be paid in the event of a breach of contract, the stated sum is known as which of the following?**

A Unliquidated damages
B Liquidated damages
C Specific damages
D Nominal damages

(2 marks)

10 **Which of the following applies to the concept of enlightened shareholder value?**

A It is the price shares can be expected to raise if they were to be sold
B It is the yardstick for assessing the performance of directors' duties
C It is the standard of behaviour expected of shareholders in general meetings

(1 mark)

11 **Which of the following involves a summary dismissal in relation to a contract of employment?**

A Both parties agree to end the contract immediately without notice
B The employee breaks the contract without notice
C The employer terminates the contract without notice

(1 mark)

 [P.T.O.

12 What qualification is the company secretary of a private limited company required to have?

    A   An appropriate legal qualification
    B   An appropriate professional qualification such as ACCA
    C   No qualification

                                      (1 mark)

13 Statutory redundancy payment is calculated on the basis of which of the following?

    A   Length of service and pay only
    B   Age and length of service only
    C   Age, length of service and pay

                                        (1 mark)

14 In relation to wrongful trading, the standard against which the conduct of directors will be assessed is which of the following?

    A   Purely subjective, depending on the actual skill of the director
    B   Purely objective, depending on what is expected of a director in that position
    C   A mixture of subjective and objective but only to increase potential liability
    D   A mixture of subjective and objective but only to reduce potential liability

                                      (2 marks)

15 Which of the following statements as regards an acceptance of an offer 'subject to contract' is true?

    A   It binds the offeror
    B   It binds neither party
    C   It binds both parties

                                        (1 mark)

16 Su had just passed her driving test when she negligently drove into a pedestrian.

    What standard of care will Su be judged by?

    A   The objective standard of a newly qualified driver, lack of experience will be taken into account
    B   The objective standard of a competent driver, lack of experience will not be taken into account
    C   The subjective standard of actual ability

                                        (1 mark)

17 Which of the following are ordinary partnerships UNABLE to create in relation to their property?

    A   Mortgages
    B   Fixed charges
    C   Floating charges

                                        (1 mark)

18 **Which of the following courts deal with civil law matters ONLY?**

A The Crown Court
B The magistrates' court
C The county court

(1 mark)

19 Jo promises to pay a reward for the return of her lost phone. Mia finds the phone and returns it to Jo.

Which of the following types of consideration has Mia provided?

A Executed consideration
B Executory consideration
C Past consideration

(1 mark)

20 **Which of the following requires court approval before the appointment of an administrator?**

A Creditors
B Holders of floating charges
C The directors of the company
D The company itself

(2 marks)

21 **Which of the following is an English court NORMALLY bound to follow?**

A An obiter statement of a higher court
B A ratio of a lower court
C A ratio of a court at the same level
D An obiter statement of the Supreme Court

(2 marks)

22 **Which of the following courts hear appeals from the magistrates' court?**

(1) County court
(2) Crown Court
(3) High Court

A (1) and (2) only
B (2) and (3) only
C (1) and (3) only
D (1), (2) and (3)

(2 marks)

23 Which of the following is NOT an automatic consequence of a compulsory winding up order against a public limited company?

A   Transfers of shareholdings are suspended
B   Liquidation is deemed to start on the date of the issuing of the order
C   Directors cease to exercise any management power
D   Employees are immediately dismissed

(2 marks)

24 Which TWO of the following apply to shares of companies whose names end in 'Ltd'?

(1)   They may not be issued to non-members
(2)   They may not be offered to the public
(3)   They may not be transferred
(4)   They may not be traded on the stock exchange

A   (1) and (2)
B   (2) and (3)
C   (1) and (4)
D   (2) and (4)

(2 marks)

25 Which of the following statements regarding the age limits for serving as a director in a public limited company is true?

A   Minimum age 16 years and no maximum age
B   Minimum age 21 years and no maximum age
C   Minimum age 21 years and maximum age 75 years
D   Minimum age 16 years and maximum age 75 years

(2 marks)

26 Which TWO of the following are private law actions?

(1)   Those between individuals
(2)   Those between business organisations
(3)   Those between individuals and the state

A   (1) and (2)
B   (1) and (3)
C   (2) and (3)

(1 mark)

27 **In which procedure does a liquidation committee operate?**

(1) Compulsory liquidation
(2) A members' voluntary liquidation
(3) A creditors' voluntary liquidation
(4) Administration

A (1) and (2)
B (2) and (4)
C (1) and (3)
D (3) and (4)

(2 marks)

28 **The category of treasury shares comes into existence under which of the following circumstances?**

A They are issued as such by a private company
B They are issued as such by a public company
C They are purchased as such by the exchequer
D They are purchased as such by a private or public company

(2 marks)

29 **Which of the following is NOT a source of English law?**

A Custom
B Equity
C Public law

(1 mark)

30 **Which of the following are owed a duty of care by auditors when preparing a company's audit report?**

A A potential investor with no current holding
B An existing shareholder looking to increase their holding
C A company looking to make a takeover bid for the company
D The company and the existing shareholders in the company as a body

(2 marks)

31 In a potential redundancy situation, an employee may lose the right to payment if they reject an offer of alternative employment within the business.

Which of the following will allow the employee to reject the employment offered and claim redundancy?

A The alternative was suitable but the employee reasonably felt that it was not of the same status
B The alternative was suitable but the employee refused to consider it
C The alternative was suitable but the employee's grounds for refusing to accept it were unreasonable

(1 mark)

[P.T.O.

32 Which TWO of the following are reasons for dismissal which must be justified as FAIR?

(1) Capability or qualifications of the employee
(2) Legal prohibitions relating to the employee
(3) Refusal of the employee to join a trade union
(4) Taking part in unofficial industrial action

A (1) and (2)
B (1) and (3)
C (2) and (3)
D (2) and (4)

(2 marks)

33 What type of contract does an employee have?

A A contract for service
B A contract of service
C A contract for services
D A contract of services

(2 marks)

34 Which of the following describes a pre-contractual statement which does NOT form a term of a contract but induces the contract?

A A condition
B A warranty
C A representation
D An innominate term

(2 marks)

35 Which of the following exists as a separate legal entity from its members?

A An ordinary partnership
B A limited partnership
C A limited liability partnership

(1 mark)

36 Which of the following must a private company ALWAYS have?

A Shares
B Limited liability
C A company secretary
D A registration certificate

(2 marks)

37 A breach of a contractual warranty enables the injured party to do which of the following?

A   To sue for damages only
B   To sue for damages or terminate the contract
C   To sue for damages and terminate the contract
D   To terminate the contract only

(2 marks)

38 In relation to the tort of negligence, which TWO of the following criteria are required to establish the existence of a duty of care?

(1)   The claimant suffered a financial loss
(2)   The harm suffered was reasonably foreseeable
(3)   A relationship of proximity existed between the parties
(4)   The claimant did not consent to cause the injury suffered

A   (1) and (2)
B   (1) and (3)
C   (2) and (3)
D   (2) and (4)

(2 marks)

39 In relation to defences to the tort of negligence, which of the following is the consequence of a finding of *volenti non fit injuria*?

A   It removes the requirement to pay damages
B   It reverses the burden of proof as to who can claim damages
C   It increases the level of damages
D   It decreases the level of damages

(2 marks)

40 Which of the following actions is open to a party who has only partly performed work under a contract?

A   Quantum meruit
B   Action for the price
C   Damages
D   Restitution

(2 marks)

41 Which of the following is an example of the purposive approach to statutory interpretation?

A   The mischief rule
B   The literal rule
C   The golden rule

(1 mark)

42 **Which is the correct minimum period of notice an employee is entitled to after five years' service?**

    A   One calendar month
    B   Five weeks
    C   Ten weeks
    D   Five calendar months

                                                                                                (2 marks)

43 **In relation to agency law, 'warrant of authority' is provided by which of the following?**

    A   The agent
    B   The principal
    C   The third party

                                                                                              (1 mark)

44 **Which of the following correctly applies to the burden of proof in a criminal case?**

    A   It must be proved beyond reasonable doubt
    B   It must be proved on the balance of probabilities
    C   It lies with the prosecution
    D   It lies with the defence

                                                                                              (2 marks)

45 **Where a business includes a term in a contract which excludes liability for death and personal injuries through negligence, which of the following states the effect of the term?**

    A   It is invalid
    B   It is invalid unless it is reasonable in the circumstances of the case
    C   It is valid only if specifically brought to the attention of the other party
    D   It is valid if it is clearly included in the contract terms

                                                                                               (2 marks)

Section B – ALL FIVE questions are compulsory and MUST be attempted

Please write your answers to all parts of these questions on the lined pages within the Candidate Answer Booklet.

1   Ann owns a shop selling prints. She placed an advertisement in the Friday edition of her local paper stating:

'Unique opportunity to own a Bell print for £500 cash. Offer valid for one day only – tomorrow Saturday.'

When Con saw the advert, he immediately posted a letter of acceptance.

On Saturday, Di asked Ann if she would take a cheque for £500, but she refused to accept the cheque and told her she could not have the print. Later that day Ann sold the print to Evi.

On Monday morning Con's letter arrived.

Required:

In the context of the rules governing the creation of contracts:

(a) Describe the precise legal nature of Ann's advertisement;   (2 marks)

(b) Explain whether Con has any right of action against Ann;   (2 marks)

(c) Explain whether Di has any right of action against Ann.   (2 marks)

                                                                                                                    (6 marks)

2   Fred is a member of Glad Ltd, a small publishing company, holding 100 of its 500 shares. The other 400 shares are held by four other members.

It has recently become apparent that Fred has set up a rival business to Glad Ltd and the other members have decided that he should be expelled from the company. To that end they propose to alter the articles of association to include a new power to 'require any member to transfer their shares for fair value to the other members upon the passing of a resolution so to do'.

Required:

(a) State the procedure which Glad Ltd must follow to alter its articles of association.   (2 marks)

(b) Explain the effect of the requirement that any alteration to a company's articles of association must be for the benefit of the company as a whole.   (2 marks)

(c) Explain whether or not the articles of association of Glad Ltd can be altered as proposed.   (2 marks)

                                                                                                                    (6 marks)

3 Three years ago Ho subscribed for shares in two companies: Ice Ltd and Jet plc. In relation to the shares in Ice Ltd, Ho was only required to pay 50 pence per £1 share when he took the shares and was assured that he would not be required to make any further payment on them to Ice Ltd and the company passed a resolution to that effect. Unfortunately, Ice Ltd has gone into insolvent liquidation owing a substantial sum of money to its creditors.

In relation to the shares in Jet plc, Ho was required to pay a premium of 50 pence per £1 share. The shares are currently trading at 75 pence per share.

Required:

(a) **Describe any potential liability Ho may have with regard to the shares he holds in Ice Ltd and to whom any such liability would be owed.** (2 marks)

(b) **Explain the meaning and purposes of a share premium account.** (2 marks)

(c) **Explain whether Ho can gain access to the premium paid on the shares in Jet plc.** (2 marks)

(6 marks)

4 Kut Ltd is a small private company. Although there are three members of its board of directors, the actual day-to-day running of the business is left to Leo, who simply reports back to the board on the business he has carried out. Leo refers to himself as the chief executive officer of Kut Ltd, although he has never been officially appointed as such.

In October 2014, Leo entered into a normal business contract on Kut Ltd's behalf with Max. However, the other members of the board have subsequently lost confidence in Leo and have refused to pay Max, claiming that Leo did not have the necessary authority to enter into the contract with him.

Required:

(a) **State the usual authority of individual directors to enter into binding contracts on behalf of their company.** (2 marks)

(b) **Explain whether or not Kut Ltd is liable to pay Max.** (4 marks)

(6 marks)

5 Nit is involved in illegal activity, from which he makes a large amount of money. He also owns a legitimate taxi company and passes off his illegally gained money as profits of that business. Nit employs Owen, who is aware of the illegal source of the money, to act as the manager of the taxi company, and Pat as his accountant to produce false business accounts for the taxi business.

Required:

In the context of the law relating to money laundering:

(a) **Explain the meaning of layering.** (2 marks)

(b) **Explain whether any criminal offences relating to money laundering may have been committed by Nit, Owen and Pat.** (4 marks)

(6 marks)

End of Question Paper

Answers

Section A

1	B
2	B
3	D
4	C
5	C
6	A
7	A
8	B
9	B
10	B
11	C
12	C
13	C
14	C
15	B
16	B
17	C
18	C
19	A
20	A
21	C
22	B
23	B
24	D
25	A
26	A
27	C
28	D
29	C
30	D
31	A
32	A
33	B
34	C
35	C
36	D
37	A
38	C
39	A
40	A
41	A
42	B
43	A
44	C
45	A

Section B

1   (a)   The first issue to determine is whether Ann's advertisement was an offer or an invitation to treat. An offer is a promise to be bound on particular terms. The offer may, through acceptance, result in a legally enforceable contract. Alternatively, an invitation to treat is an invitation to others to make offers. The person extending the invitation is not bound to accept any offers made to them. Usually, advertisements only amount to an invitation to treat and cannot be accepted to form a binding contract (*Partridge* v *Crittenden* (1968)). There are occasions, however, when an advert can amount to a genuine offer capable of acceptance by anyone to whom the offer is addressed (*Carlill* v *Carbolic Smoke Ball Co* (1893)). The wording of Ann's advert was in sufficiently categorical terms for it to have been an offer to the world at large, stating her unreserved commitment to enter into a contract with the first person who accepted it.

   (b)   Once an offeree accepts the terms offered, a contract comes into effect and both parties are bound.

   Usually, acceptance must be communicated to the offeror. However, there are exceptions, one of which arises where acceptance is through the postal service. In the latter circumstances, acceptance is complete as soon as the letter, properly

15

addressed and stamped, is posted (*Adams* v *Lindsell* (1818)). The postal rule will only apply, however, where it is in the contemplation of the parties that the post will be used as the means of acceptance.

Con has clearly tried to accept the offer but his reliance on the postal rule would be to no avail as the use of the post was clearly an inappropriate mode of acceptance. He, therefore, has no right of action against Ann.

(c) In order to form a binding agreement, acceptance must correspond with the terms of the offer. Thus the offeree must not seek to introduce new contractual terms into their acceptance (*Neale* v *Merritt* (1830)). Any attempt to do so amounts to a counter-offer and leaves the original offeror at liberty to accept or reject the new offer as they choose (*Hyde* v *Wrench* (1840)).

Ann's advertisement clearly stated that she wanted cash for the print and, therefore, Di's attempt to pay with a cheque did not comply with the original offer and leaves her with no grounds for complaint. The decision in *D & C Builders Ltd* v *Rees* (1966) as to cheques being equivalent to money is not to the point, as Ann wanted immediate payment for the print.

2 **(a)** Section 21 Companies Act 2006 provides for the alteration of articles of association by the passing of a special resolution, requiring a 75% vote in favour of the proposition. Consequently, the directors of Glad Ltd must call a general meeting of the company and put forward a resolution to alter the articles as proposed. Fred will be entitled to attend the meeting, speak and vote on the resolution.

If the resolution is successful, a copy of the new articles must be sent to the Companies Registry within 15 days.

(b) Any such alteration, as is proposed, has to be made '*bona fide* in the interest of the company as a whole'. This test involves a subjective element, in that those deciding the alteration must actually believe they are acting in the interest of the company. There is additionally, however, an objective element requiring that any alteration has to be in the interest of the 'individual hypothetical member' (*Greenhalgh* v *Arderne Cinemas Ltd* (1951)). Whether any alteration meets this requirement depends on the facts of the particular case. In *Brown* v *British Abrasive Wheel Co Ltd* (1919), an alteration to a company's articles to allow the 98% majority to buy out the 2% minority shareholders was held to be invalid as not being in the interest of the company as a whole. However, in *Sidebottom* v *Kershaw Leese & Co* (1920), an alteration to the articles to give the directors the power to require any shareholder, who entered into competition with the company, to sell their shares to nominees of the directors at a fair price was held to be valid.

(c) It is extremely likely that the alteration will be permitted. Fred only controls 20% of the voting power in the company and so he is no position to prevent the passing of the necessary special resolution to alter the articles as proposed. Additionally, it would clearly benefit the company as a whole, and the hypothetical individual shareholder, to prevent Fred from competing with the company, so Fred would lose any challenge he subsequently raised in court.

3 **(a)** There is no requirement that companies should require their shareholders to immediately pay the full value of the shares. The proportion of the nominal value of the issued capital actually paid by the shareholder is called the paid up capital. It may be the full nominal value, in which case it fulfils the shareholder's responsibility to the company; or it can be a mere part payment, in which case the company has an outstanding claim against the shareholder. It is possible for a company to pass a resolution that it will not make a call on any unpaid capital. However, even in this situation, the unpaid element can be called upon if the company cannot pay its debts from existing assets in the event of its liquidation.

Applying this to Ho's case, it can be seen that he has a maximum potential liability in relation to his shares in Ice Ltd of 50 pence per share. The exact amount of his liability will depend on the extent of the company's debts but it will be fixed at a maximum of 50 pence per share.

(b) It is common for successful companies to issue shares at a premium, the premium being the value received over and above the nominal value of the shares. Section 610 Companies Act 2006 provides that any such premium received must be placed into a share premium account. The premium obtained is regarded as equivalent to capital and, as such, there are limitations on how the fund can be used. Section 130 provides that the share premium account can be used for the following purposes:

(i)   to pay up bonus shares to be allotted as fully paid to members;
(ii)   to write off preliminary expenses of the company;
(iii)   to write off the expenses, commission or discount incurred in any issue of shares or debentures of the company;
(iv)   to pay for the premium payable on redemption of debentures.

(c) Applying the rules relating to capital maintenance, it follows that the share premium account cannot be used for payments to the shareholders.

Applying the rules to Ho's situation, it can be seen that he cannot get any of the premium paid for the shares in Jet plc back from the company in the form of cash.

Ho would not even be able to recover the money indirectly as the shares are currently trading at below the nominal value, and at half of the premium price he paid.

4 **(a)** This question requires candidates to consider the authority of company directors to enter into binding contracts on behalf of their companies.

Article 3 of the model articles of association for private companies provides that the directors of a company may exercise all the powers of the company. It is important to note that this power is given to the board as a whole and not to individual directors and consequently individual directors cannot bind the company without their being authorised, in some way, so to do.

(b) There are three ways in which the power of the board of directors may be extended to individual directors.

(i) The individual director may be given express authority to enter into a particular transaction on the company's behalf. To this end, Article 5 allows for the delegation of the board's powers to one or more directors. Where such express delegation has been made, then the company is bound by any contract entered into by the person to whom the power was delegated.

(ii) A second type of authority which may empower an individual director to bind his company is implied authority. In this situation, the person's authority flows from their position. The mere fact of appointment to a particular position will mean that the person so appointed will have the implied authority to bind the company to the same extent as people in that position usually do (*Hely-Hutchinson* v *Brayhead Ltd* (1968)).

(iii) The third way in which an individual director may possess the power to bind his company is through the operation of ostensible authority, which is alternatively described as apparent authority or agency by estoppel. This arises where an individual director has neither express nor implied authority. Nonetheless, the director is held out by the other members of the board of directors as having the authority to bind the company. If a third party acts on such a representation, then the company will be estopped from denying its truth (*Freeman and Lockyer* v *Buckhurst Park Properties (Mangal) Ltd* (1964)).

The situation in the problem is very similar to that in *Freeman and Lockyer* v *Buckhurst Park Properties (Mangal) Ltd*. The board of Kut Ltd has permitted Leo to act as its chief executive, and he has even used that title. The board has therefore acquiesced in his representation of himself as their chief executive and consequently Kut Ltd is bound by any contracts he might make within the scope of a chief executive's implied authority. As the contract in question is in the ordinary run of business, it would clearly come within that authority. Consequently Kut Ltd will be liable to pay Max or face an action for breach of contract.

5 **(a)** Money laundering is a criminal offence under the Proceeds of Crime Act (POCA) 2002. Layering is one of the stages in the overall process of money laundering designed to disguise the illegal source of money. It involves the transfer of money made from illegal sources from place to place and from one business to another in order to conceal the initial illegal source of the money. The layering process may involve many inter-business transfers in an attempt to confuse any potential investigation of the original source of the money.

(b) The POCA 2002 seeks to control money laundering by creating three categories of criminal offences in relation to that activity.

– **laundering**
The principal money laundering offence relates to laundering the proceeds of crime or assisting in that process. Under s.327, it is an offence to conceal, disguise, convert, transfer or remove criminal property.

– **failure to report**
The second category of offence relates to failing to report a knowledge or suspicion of money laundering. Under s.330 POCA 2002 it is an offence for a person who knows or suspects that another person is engaged in money laundering not to report the fact to the appropriate authority.

– **tipping off**
The third category of offence relates to tipping off. Section 333 POCA 2002 makes it an offence to make a disclosure, which is likely to prejudice any investigation under the Act.

It is apparent from the scenario that all three people involved in the scenario are liable to prosecution under the POCA 2002 as they are involved in money laundering. If the original money to establish the taxi company was the product of crime, then that transaction itself was an instance of money laundering. However, even if that were not the case and the taxi company had been bought from legitimate money, it is nonetheless the case that it is being used to conceal the fact that the source of much of Nit's money is criminal activity.

Nit would therefore be guilty on the primary offence of money laundering under s.327 POCA 2002.

Whether or not Owen is also guilty of an offence in relation to the POCA depends on the extent of his knowledge as to what is actually going on in the company. As he knows what is taking place, then, as he is clearly assisting Nit in his money laundering procedure, his activity is covered by s.327, as he is actively concealing and disguising criminal property. He would also be liable under s.328 as his arrangement with Nit 'facilitates the retention of criminal property'.

Pat is also guilty under the same provisions as Owen, in that he is actively engaged in the money laundering process, by producing false accounts. Had he not been an active party to the process, he might nonetheless have been liable, under s.330, for failing to disclose any suspiciously high profits from the taxi business.

Section A

1–45   One or two marks per question, total marks 70

Section B

1   This question requires an explanation of the rules relating to the formation of contracts, especially the distinction between offers and invitations to treat and the rules of acceptance of offers.

(a)   2 marks   Good analysis and explanation of the nature of Ann's advertisement.
1 mark   Some explanation, but lacking in detail or application.
0 marks   No knowledge whatsoever of the topic.

(b)   2 marks   A good explanation of Con's situation in law.
1 mark   Some, but limited, explanation.
0 marks   No knowledge or explanation.

(c)   2 marks   A good explanation of Di's situation in law.
1 mark   Some, but limited, explanation.
0 marks   No knowledge or explanation.

2   This question requires an explanation of the rules relating to the alteration of a company's articles of association generally. It also requires an understanding of the way in which individual shareholders can have their right expropriated.

(a)   2 marks   Good analysis and explanation of the procedure for altering articles of association.
1 mark   Some explanation, but lacking in detail or application.
0 marks   No knowledge whatsoever of the topic.

(b)   2 marks   Good explanation of what is meant by in the interest of the company as a whole.
1 mark   Some explanation, but lacking in detail or application.
0 marks   No knowledge whatsoever of the topic.

(c)   2 marks   Good analysis of the likely outcome with reasons.
1 mark   Some explanation, but lacking in detail or application.
0 marks   No knowledge whatsoever of the topic.

3   This question requires an explanation of the rules relating to shareholders' liability for shares.

(a)   2 marks   Good analysis and explanation of the nature of Ho's potential liability.
1 mark   Some explanation, but lacking in detail or application.
0 marks   No knowledge whatsoever of the topic.

(b)   2 marks   A good explanation of the share premium account and what it can be used for.
1 mark   Some, but limited, explanation.
0 marks   No knowledge or explanation.

(c)   2 marks   A good explanation of Ho's inability to access the share premium account.
1 mark   Some, but limited, explanation.
0 marks   No knowledge or explanation.

4   This question requires a consideration of the powers of individual directors to bind their company in contracts.

(a)   2 marks   Good explanation of the directors' powers collectively and individually.
1 mark   Some explanation, but lacking in detail or application.
0 marks   No knowledge whatsoever of the topic.

(b)   3–4 marks   A good explanation of express, implied and apparent authority plus appropriate application of that knowledge.
1–2 marks   Some, but limited, explanation or application.
0 marks   No knowledge or explanation.

5 This question requires a consideration of the law relating to money laundering.

(a) 2 marks   Good explanation of the process of layering in the context of money laundering.
1 mark   Some explanation, but lacking in detail or application.
0 marks   No knowledge whatsoever of the topic.

(b) 3–4 marks   A good explanation of the potential crimes under the Proceeds of Crime Act 2002 plus appropriate application of that knowledge.
1–2 marks   Some, but limited, explanation or application.
0 marks   No knowledge or explanation.

ABOUT BECKER PROFESSIONAL EDUCATION

Becker Professional Education provides a single solution for students and professionals looking to advance their careers and achieve success in:

- Accounting

- International Financial Reporting

- Project Management

- Continuing Professional Education

- Healthcare

For more information on how Becker Professional Education can support you in your career, visit www.becker.com/acca.

Becker Professional Education
is an ACCA approved content provider